STEPPING STONES
FOR
STUMBLING SAINTS

Robin Wentworth Mayer

faithQuest® • *Brethren Press*®
Elgin, Illinois

To the many people who kept saying to me,
"You ought to write a book!"

TABLE OF CONTENTS

I. When You've Walked
on Water and Sunk...
Overcoming fear, failure, and feelings of inadequacy

II. When You've Wandered
from the Path of Righteousness...
Learning from mistakes

III. When You've Fallen
and Can't Get Up...
Growing through painful experiences

IV. When You Trip on the Tie that Binds...
Working toward healthy relationships

V. When You Come to a Crossroads...
Making changes and accepting limitations

VI. Toward Higher Ground...
Setting your mind on things above

*A version of this article first appeared in *Messenger* magazine.

PREFACE

I get headaches in the self-help sections of Christian bookstores. All those titles promising "triumphant Christian living" feel more like indictment than inspiration to me. I rarely finish a how-to book. Generally I find them to be superficial in content and simplistic in outlook. To be truthful, I've been mad at Oprah Winfrey ever since she lost all that weight. I could forgive her for *losing* it, but I resent the peptalks. I get so disgusted with the pat answers and empty platitudes I hear on radio talk shows I'd call in and challenge them if I weren't afraid someone would recognize my voice and tell my kids, causing them cruel and unusual embarrassment.

I don't mean to sound cynical. It's just that when I'm struggling I don't want a coach or a cheerleader—I want a *companion*. And I know that a lot of struggling believers feel the same way.

I have two degrees in psychology, but I didn't write *Stepping Stones* to do counseling. I graduated from seminary magna cum laude, but *Stepping Stones* is not a theological treatise. I've been a pastor for nearly ten years, but *Stepping Stones* contains little that could be called preaching.

Stepping Stones for Stumbling Saints is a collection of conversational essays that illustrates familiar ways we all stumble in the walk of faith and then offers suggestions (i.e., stepping stones) to help you regain your footing. If you're somebody who doesn't stumble, or doesn't admit to stumbling, simply put the book down and walk away quickly. No one will ever know. Likewise, if you're looking for a quick fix or a one-size-fits-all solution, you'd better look somewhere else.

Stepping Stones won't give you all the answers to all your questions or solve all your problems. But I hope it will give you a place to pause and consider the questions as well as some fresh insight to the practical ways that Scripture applies to life.

I | WHEN YOU'VE WALKED ON WATER AND SUNK...

Overcoming fear, failure, and feelings of inadequacy

SCALING MOUNTAINS

I've worked in the helping professions my entire adult life: as a juvenile probation officer just out of college, as a therapist for several years after completing my graduate work, and currently as a pastor. Which all goes to say that over the years I've been involved with countless individuals struggling with heartbreaking, gut-wrenching, spirit-crushing problems. And while the details, circumstances, personalities, social status, and genders differ, a common theme runs through each situation: They feel overwhelmed with despair and can see no light at the end of the tunnel.

Whatever the problem, whatever the solution, whatever the strategy, I'm convinced that the surest route to frustration is to expect too much and travel too fast. The unfortunate backwash of our competitive, high-performance culture is a mind-set that believes the sky is the limit and the deadline was yesterday.

A few years ago I helped chaperone a "Wandering Wheels" youth trip to Florida via Gatlinburg. Part of the planned agenda in those Great Smoky Mountains was to climb the Chimney Tops peaks. Not up the path like typical tourists, mind you. We were to scale up the back.

At first I felt challenged and a little smug, sure that I would have no trouble keeping up with those kids who were fifteen to twenty years younger than I. However, somewhere about halfway up, all my confidence and cockiness evaporated. I have never feared for my life as I did on that cold, sunny, slippery mountainside. Later, the teenagers who were with me never grew tired of telling others how white my face became.

But here's what I noticed: Every time I tilted my head back and focused on the top of the mountain, I felt dizzy and weak—totally paralyzed with fear. But when I simply concentrated on the next foothold, the next handhold, the next stepping stone, I was able to slowly, surely climb over the top. A good portion of the journey was made on my backside, but I got there.

We are all wounded people at best. If the scars on our psyches were visible to the human eye, some of us would be a scary sight indeed. The discouraging word is that life is beset with trials and troubles. We will always have unanticipated problems, disappointing setbacks, unrealized dreams, high demands, and low thresholds.

But the good news is that we don't have to be perfect, cater to every demand, cover every base, or achieve every goal. Whoever told you that you have to be superhuman to be successful, lied. When it comes to managing life's difficulties, we don't need to walk on water; we just need to learn where the stepping stones are.

Brown-Eyed Angels

When I was little I was never selected to be an angel in the Christmas program. I've been Mary, I've been a shepherd, I've been a wiseman...seems like one year I was even the back half of a camel!

But the angels' roles were usually reserved for the little girls with blonde curls, fair skin, and blue eyes. I can remember drooling with envy over the tinsel halos and chiffon wings they got to wear while I trudged around in somebody's bathrobe. I also remember feeling unlucky, unspecial, unfavored...in a word, unworthy.

The experiences of childhood make their mark. Now, nobody set out to hurt me; mine was just one of countless situations where stereotypes were left unquestioned, and consequently feelings were overlooked. And while this was undoubtedly not the only factor hampering the development of my self-esteem, it left an indelible impression.

Through the years as I've read Christmas stories to my son, watched Christmas pageants on TV, or assigned parts for church Christmas programs, I still cringe if there are no dark-haired, brown-eyed angels represented among the heavenly host. Not surprisingly, in my favorite Christmas stories the one who isn't "good enough" gets chosen as the very best—you know, like Rudolph the Red-Nosed Reindeer and Tazewell's Littlest Angel.

Those who know me well can attest to the fact that I am a hopeless champion of the underdog. And yes, all this certainly influenced my decision to pursue careers of counseling and ministry. It has nothing to do with pity or duty. It has to do with *identification*.

Likewise, it is the same sense of identification that brought God to Bethlehem. You see, he could have burst into our stratosphere on a lightning bolt, swooped through like Superman, beamed down like Captain Kirk, or exploded in like Rambo. And had God penetrated the space-time continuum in such dramatic fashion, he still could have accomplished the primary objective of redemption.

But then he would have bypassed the kinds of life experiences that would have caused him to understand what it's like to be the one on the playground the other kids make fun of...the last one chosen for sandlot baseball...the only one without a date for the school dance...the one ignored by scholarship committees...the one passed over for a promotion...or the one not selected as an angel in the Christmas play. If it weren't for Bethlehem, Jesus could not identify with our inadequacies, with our hang-ups, with our rejections, with all the things past, present, and future that make us feel we don't quite measure up.

The manger is a mystery with many messages. But the one that speaks to me most clearly is that Jesus *identifies* with all of us who know what it is like to be second choice, second string, and second fiddle.

Yes, he atoned for sin. Yes, he fulfilled the law. Yes, he defeated Satan. Yes, he made possible eternal life. And yes, he did many other theological things that none of us understand as well as we think we do.

But in addition to all of that, Christ's advent also brings the promise of value to the worthless, purpose to the aimless, confidence to the confused, and significance to the obscure. For those willing to believe, there are no further qualifications, no prerequisites, no auditions, no screenings, and (thank God) no cuts.

Next Christmas as you look into the faces of your friends, neighbors, and children—perhaps even as you look at the one gazing back in your mirror—keep in mind that some angels have brown eyes.

Like Riding a Bicycle

For his fifth birthday, my son received a brand-new bicycle with training wheels. After several months of assisted riding, he seemed ready to have them taken off.

Jameson quickly learned to balance himself but immediately discovered that unassisted starting and stopping were far more difficult. After his first few attempts ended in panic-induced wipe-outs he elected to simply retire his bike.

Nearly a year later, Jameson still couldn't ride that bike. And instead of his fear gradually abating, it was escalating to phobic proportions. Deciding that he was big enough, old enough, coordinated enough, and smart enough to master the skills required to ride a bicycle, I took a calculated risk one evening and insisted he accompany me on a bike ride.

I'll never forget it. His adrenaline must've been in overdrive, because he had no trouble keeping pace. And as I glanced over at him, the trembling lower lip, white-knuckled little hands and fear-glazed eyes nearly sent *me* into an emotional wipe-out! I worried and wondered: *Did I push too hard? Did he need more time?*

He finished the course, but not without mishap. While the worst of his irrational fears did not materialize, the bumps and bruises were certainly real enough. What now?

The next morning my misgivings evaporated as I heard Jameson bragging to his grandma how far he'd ridden his bike "...without any training wheels and with only one crash!"

This is not about riding bicycles. This is about fear—because many of us live with irrational fears that restrain and confine us. They lurk in the shadows of our choices, spying out our liberty and keeping us in bondage. And what is important to understand is that sometimes we cannot navigate *around* a fear, but instead must ride *through* it.

How? With the *Triple A Travel Guide*.

First of all, ACKNOWLEDGE your fear. Don't try to talk yourself out of it. Denial is to fear as dampness is to fungus.

Then, ANALYZE your fear. What situations trigger it? When do you feel it? How does it affect your behavior? What is its source? Whom do you run from or turn to when you feel it? Does it pose a realistic danger?

Finally, ACT...and act in a manner that is consistent with your goals, regardless of your fears. There will be times when your fear serves as the guardian angel of your standards and values. Thus the fear will be a friend to your goals.

However, there will be many, many times that your fears latch onto your personality like a parasite, limiting your options and draining your potential. And if you wait for your fear to disappear *before* you act, the odds are better than even that you'll never act. Once you act, you'll find out that mastering a fear is like riding a bicycle; once you do it, you never forget how.

After I insisted my son give up his training wheels, he began riding his bicycle with the unconscious confidence of legions of boys before him—popping wheelies, weaving in and out of parked cars, and dodging chuckholes. Hands optional, of course. It is easy to see that in mastering his fear, he widened his world.

So can you.

Losing Weight, Gaining Ground

I have a friend. Actually I have many friends. But this particular friend has carried around almost twice as much weight as she needs for many years. All the time I have known her, in fact. She is, by medical as well as cosmetic standards, obese.

Like most female friends, we'd often discuss dieting and weight loss (usually over dessert!). But it was heartbreakingly obvious to all who knew her that Karen had little follow-through on her good intentions. Until recently.

She called me several weeks ago to share that she had joined a well-known, highly effective weight loss program and had already shed sixteen pounds. Karen's tears are never far from the surface, so it was no time before we were both sniffling and blubbering into the phone (some people are social drinkers; I'm a social crier!). But two things she said to me that day ring over and over again in my ears, and I believe they provide powerful insight into a broad spectrum of problems, not just obesity.

"I just never realized how fat I was."

So often we are blind to our problem even though it may be apparent to others. This is why it's so important to listen to the feedback of people who love us without bristling and defending. They may very well see something we're missing about ourselves. If I stretch out my arm and hold a mirror in my hand, I can only see a portion of myself. Let someone else take that same mirror and step back several feet and, like magic, all of me comes into view.

The flip side, of course, is that it's important to *give* constructive feedback to those we love. And remember that *love* is the qualifying word here. We have not earned the right to offer such feedback until we have communicated unconditional love.

"I finally admitted I couldn't do it alone."

Does that have a familiar ring? The launching pad for the Twelve Steps of A.A. is: "We admitted we were powerless." It takes both humility and courage to ask for help. So with that admission, Karen was on her way to recovery. No matter how feeble the gesture, reaching out is the turning point towards victory, recovery, healing, and success—you choose the adjective.

When we met for lunch the other day, Karen and I had salad, which provides another clue to progress: We must make choices consistent with our goals. It is not easy to dismantle a way of life. It is painful; it is tedious; it is indescribably difficult. We can accomplish it only by directing each small step toward our ultimate destination.

Six months into her program (and almost fifty pounds lighter) Karen divulged to me her starting weight, a secret I thought she would carry to her grave. But here's what I noticed: Courage takes risks, which increases confidence, which enables greater risks, which in turn leads to more confidence—and so on and so on. As we follow this pattern our self-esteem goes spinning to new heights in an upward spiral.

Those of us who grew up watching *Superman* reruns and old *Tarzan* movies are programmed to measure courage in terms of dangerous confrontations, daring escapes, and dashing rescues. But I'm inclined to believe that the greatest courage is demonstrated by people like Karen—people who bravely (which is not the same as fearlessly) elect to do battle with themselves. Whether the problem be obesity, addiction, depression, or _____ (fill in the blank) the healing process alters little: Admit the problem, reach for help, keep choices consistent with goals, and take confidence-building risks.

Cookie Confessions

Sunday Morning, 10:00 a.m....

My turn to help with the once-a-month fellowship break. I watched with hungry eyes as the young adult class set out dozens of picture-perfect home-baked cookies. Temptation beckoned, but I prevailed.

Same day, high noon...

Joined the senior high youth for their meeting. The cookies were back, and they had only grown more lovely with age. Enticing, but I resisted.

That afternoon, 2:00 p.m....

Finally arrived home, alone. Checked the e-mail, changed clothes, made a phone call, let the dog out, ate a dozen cookies, read the paper.

Later, 4:00 p.m....

Accompanied family to the church skating party where I ignored the cookies as if willpower could retroactively expunge my dastardly deed. Daintily I nibbled on low-fat veggies, hoping no one would notice the scarlet "C" on my chest.

No one did. God did not zap me. Friends did not forsake me. My secret indulgence brought neither shame nor ridicule.

Isn't it funny how we fool ourselves into thinking that the things we do in secret will not count against us? As long as no one knows...as long as no one gets hurt...as long as I don't cause anyone else to stumble...as long as I keep faith with other commitments...as long as it's *just this once....*

The problem is, though, as long as it remains hidden, it is never just this once: "When that desire has conceived, it gives birth to sin, and that sin, when it is fully grown, gives birth to death" (James 1:15).

A married woman becomes enamored with another man. Lust is conceived. While they transgress no physical boundaries, she attaches to him emotionally the soul that belongs to another. Sin is accomplished. As a result she no longer "feels anything" for the husband to whom she promised faithfulness. A marriage dies.

A man becomes dissatisfied with his work routine and longs for the power and status of his superiors. Lust is conceived. He begins to report luncheon meetings with bogus clients and pads his expense account. Sin is accomplished. He's not as smart as he thinks he is, so when his infraction is discovered, he's fired. A career dies.

A teenager resents his parents' rules and envies his friends who have none. Lust is conceived. So one night he lies to Mom and Dad in order to sneak over to a friend's older brother's apartment. Sin is accomplished. They drink beer and watch porno movies till dawn. Innocence dies.

A person who has resolved to lose weight begins to feel cheated because others do not have the same battle. Lust is conceived. She maintains a front publicly, but in secret makes choices that are diametrically opposed to her goals. Sin is accomplished. It only takes a few such scenarios for her to feel like a total failure. Hope dies.

Every time we begin to resent something about our current situation and tell ourselves "I *deserve better!*" we've allowed lust to be conceived. After that, choices contrary to our standards and commitments (i.e., sin) follow much more easily. Then when sin is accomplished, something dies.

And it's not always a physical death. More often it's the death of a relationship...the death of wonder...the death of trust...the death of integrity...the death of a dream.

That's why James also says: "Confess your sins to one another...so that you may be healed" (James 5:16). Lust can only grow in darkness. Sin can only prevail in secrecy. Confession brings it into the Light where lust's power is neutralized and sin's appeal is weakened. Which in turn sets us free to makes choices that lead not to death, but to life.

SKATES, SKIS, AND SHIPS

Skating is not new to me. I grew up in the church, and roller-skating was one of the few recreational activities that was considered wholesome (I guess no one noticed how similar it was to dancing!).

So, once a month my parents, brothers, and I used to go skating with our church fellowship group. It was tremendous fun. We were allowed to stay up past 9:00 p.m., and my dad taught us to skate backwards, cross-over around the corners, and hokey-pokey without missing a beat.

But recently when I made my once-a-year foray onto the roller rink during our church's annual skating party, I was surprised at how wobbly I felt. What had changed? Did a year's aging make that much difference? Was I heavier? Weaker? Had something happened to my sense of balance? Tentatively I skated a few laps, then spent the rest of the afternoon spectating. It was as I was watching the kids race around at breakneck speed that I realized what they had that I'd lost: They weren't afraid of falling.

When I was in college, I learned to ski the hard way—by ignoring the beginner's slope and heading straight for the chair lift. Before I could even stand steady, I was barreling down the hill. I was enthusiastic, adventurous, and perhaps a little stupid. Those first few times, I took more creative spills than I could possibly count. But you know what? I learned to ski.

Eventually though, I became reluctant to appear foolish...I got tired of bumps and bruises...I grew embarrassed by my mistakes...and I began to fear falling.

One of the silent tragedies of human experience is the person who goes through life as though the only item on the agenda is to avoid mistakes. It's silent because there are no major failures to draw attention. It's tragic because failure-free living is acquired at the expense of growth and fulfillment.

In his book, *The Psychology of Religion*, Wayne E. Oates discusses three approaches to morality for dealing with the choices, temptations, and dreams of life.

He calls the first a "morality of safety." This is the approach that assumes that a mistake, any mistake, is the equivalent of the "unforgivable sin." Thus the best approach is to avoid risk at all cost.

The second is the flip side, a "morality of neglect." Here all caution is thrown to the wind and potential problems denied. You can imagine the resulting chaos.

Oates's third, and recommended approach, is a "morality of calculated risk." This attitude assumes that human life must be tested under careful conditions of freedom in the same way a ship has to be given a shakedown cruise. And by collaborating with others in calculating the risks of a situation, we move towards reality, responsibility, and fulfillment.

Take inventory of your life. Are you forfeiting legitimate opportunities because they also contain temptations? Have you aborted a possibility because it included a pitfall? Have you declined a challenge for fear of failure? Have you thrown the baby out with the bath?

Living is risky business to be sure. But taking calculated risks is the only path to growth. One of my all-time favorite quotes is from Charlie Shedd: "A ship in harbor is safe…but that is not what ships are made for."

Like skating and skiing, living can only be done well when we get over our fear of falling.

THE SHOEMAKER'S KIDS

You remember the shoemaker's kids, don't you? The ones who go barefoot? I often consider the chilling implications of that old adage for the minister's son.

Of all the jobs I do, of all the hats I wear, of all the roles I play, of all the people I am, I consider no task or commission as high and as holy as parenting. I also consider nothing else as difficult or as scary.

Most challenges I can meet without so much as flinching. Do you have sullen, rebellious teenagers? Send 'em my way. A married couple seething with hostilities? I can help. Want me to write a thesis? Anytime. Organize a major conference? No problem. Preach before a large assembly heavily populated with individuals who believe women should not be in the pulpit? I'm ready when you are. What's that? I'm supposed to be gentle, firm, patient, understanding, and consistent with my preschooler? Lord have mercy!

I suspect that kids are mysteriously programmed with a primitive instinct that drives them towards the ultimate goal of making their parents feel like failures. During my younger years I foolishly thought this didn't surface until adolescence. I now know that it begins to assert itself as soon as they are capable of understanding what we want. Because then, you see, it is a simple matter of doing the opposite.

I didn't allow my son to have toy guns. That's not necessarily a political statement on my part. I just don't think guns are a playing matter. So what did Jameson do? He created "gungs" out of his toy flute, Lincoln logs, or anything else with a barrel. And when he would "shoot" he usually aimed directly at me. Somehow I can't convince myself that's mere coincidence! I have this nightmarish fantasy that someday he'll take a semiautomatic weapon on a wild shooting spree. Then when he's apprehended and questioned as to why he did it, he'll reply, "My mother never let me play with guns when I was little." So I worry that he's going barefoot.

As you might expect, I worked toward minimizing sex-role stereotyping. I changed the wording of stories as I read to him, I employed inclusive language as much as possible, and we talked about the things that *both* boys and girls could do. Then one day while he was yet three years old, I commented that I needed a ladder to change a light bulb. Jameson informed me that "wadies don't use wadders, mens use wadders." *Who's been indoctrinating my child behind my back?!* Bone of my bone, flesh of my flesh, fruit of my womb...and I wondered, *Is he going barefoot?*

I'd explain consequences of choices to him and reasons for restrictions, beginning with good intentions of listening through his objections. But as the whining and resistance would escalate, my composure would disintegrate and I'd snap, "Just SHUT UP!" And immediately I feel the Sword pierce my soul. For in that instant, I *knew* he was going barefoot.

So I'd ask myself the question that parents have asked for generations: Am I doing anything right? Yes...yes, I think so. I'm loving him.

I'd observe him in the laboratory of life interacting with people. He expects to be liked and accepted by whomever he meets and has yet to encounter a stranger he could not charm into attentiveness and engage in conversation. With children he is considerate, with adults he is cooperative. He is bright, winsome, and gregarious. He is also independent, strong-willed, and demanding. We have our battles, and we have our moments. Is *this* shoemaker's kid going barefoot? I'm afraid some days he does.

But then I comfort myself with the same proverb (quoted by more than one New Testament writer) that I use to encourage other parents: "Love covers a multitude of sins" (1 Peter 4:8). If *sin* literally means "to miss the mark," then love is able to close the gap between my imperfect aim and the bull's-eye.

So to all mothers and fathers who face their parenting responsibilities with guilt, confusion, and anxiety, take heart. Nobody has all the answers...not even the so-called experts. Love covers a multitude of *mistakes* and is able to compensate where we lack. I'm trusting it will be more than adequate to make up for those barefoot days.

GOING BATTY

It was storming outside.

My sleep-sogged mental state registered that fact as my entire body protested the invasion of slumber. I squinted at my digital clock, which was blinking at me like a neon sign: *Good, only 3:00 a.m.* That left nearly three hours till the alarm would go off. I snuggled down into the blankets and let my mind drift off to the midnight music of the abating storm.

Outside, the wind was now whooshing instead of howling, the thunder rumbled rather than cracked, the lightning was a fading flicker, and the rain pattered gently against the window. Inside, the drone of the fan provided background noise for the rhythmic flapping of bat wings above my head...

BAT WINGS ABOVE MY HEAD!!!

There is a phrase used several times in the Old Testament to describe the total evaporation of spirit and courage: "Their hearts melted within them." I understand exactly how it feels to have your heart melt within you. I shriveled beneath the covers and peered into the darkness, straining to separate form from shadow. Silently I pleaded, *Please, God, don't let it be true!*

But it was true. I saw the creature circling and swooping, trying in vain to exit from whence it came.

For several minutes I lay there frozen, absolutely terrified and not at all convinced that the supposedly harmless little rodent would not suddenly transform into a ghoulish character who'd say, "I vant to drink your blood!"

Where, oh, where are all the knights in shining armor when you need them?

I only knew of one way to get rid of a bat. And I knew if I didn't act soon it would vanish into some invisible crevice in the wall only to materialize later.

Somehow I started moving. I crawled out of bed. Then I crawled over to the door. (Literally. I wasn't about to put my head in the vicinity of a bat's flight path.) Closing the door behind me to keep IT confined, I found the old tennis racquet.

Upon reentering the room, I dropped back to my knees and used the racquet to push the light switch up. There IT was, crawling out of a box on the top of my bureau. Its ugly little face seemed to be sneering all kinds of unprintable bat names at me.

It started flying again.

Still on my knees, I swung the tennis racquet every time it dipped within range. I'm not a particularly good aim with my eyes *open*, let alone closed. But I kept trying, and eventually the law of averages prevailed. Staving off the cat, I gingerly scooped one mortally wounded bat into a plastic bag. Quenching the urge to drive a silver stake through its heart and bury it with a silver cross, I took it outside to the trash and briefly considered hanging a wreath of garlic on my door.

The first time I wrote about this experience was in the small town where the incident occurred. Since most residents there knew what it was like to have an uninvited bat in their home, they roared with laughter. The second time I wrote about it some of the readers roared—but not with laughter.

Was killing the bat the best thing I could have done? Maybe not. But at that particular point in time it was the best I could do with the resources available.

Fear does funny things to us. It sets us up for superstitious thinking. It narrows our perspective. It shortens our list of options. It can drive us batty. Somehow in that process, for me, overcoming the fear became the primary issue.

Fear, whether it is rational or not, has to be confronted— and defeated. I had a supervisor who used to say, "Anything worth doing is worth doing poorly." Nobody gets everything right the first time. But when a fear has reached phobic proportions, you have only two choices: You can either master it—or let it master you.

Running "Bandit"

Several years and pounds ago (you don't need to know how many), I ran a lot of road races. And in the beginning I often ran them "bandit." In other words, instead of paying the registration fee, receiving a number, and being official, I'd hop in at the back of the pack and veer off just before the finish line.

It wasn't exactly allowed. But then, it wasn't exactly forbidden either. I figured: Why pay a fee when I can run the same course and get the same benefits for nothing? After a while though, I quit running bandit and started running legal. Here's why.

My conscience got to me first. It takes an incredible amount of work by many volunteers to organize a ten-, fifteen-, or twenty-kilometer race: pre-race publicity and mailings, registration forms, water stations, statisticians, timers, first aid, post-race refreshments, and of course, the T-shirts. Nobody was getting rich off the seven-dollar registration fees. I decided that if I intended to reap the benefits of the races, I needed to take an active part in supporting them.

Secondly, I noticed that as a bandit runner, I never quite felt a part of the group. There's a peculiar camaraderie and post-race bonding that occurs among runners. Everywhere tired, aching, sweaty runners are re-agonizing over every hill and reliving every turn. Something about not being named on the roster left me on the outside looking in.

Thirdly, I got in touch with the real reason I was not paying the registration fee—which had absolutely nothing to do with my budget. I came to realize that the primary reason I didn't officially join the race was because deep down inside, I felt I didn't deserve to.

I am neither athletically gifted nor competitively minded. Therefore when it comes to sports, any sport, I've never excelled. When I ran road races I didn't win. I didn't place. I didn't set any records. Basically, I believed my running wasn't good enough to merit joining, so I felt my running didn't count for anything.

And I suggest to you, dear reader, that the above reasons have a lot to do with why many of you do not join your local church congregation, and why many others who have joined remain on the fringes.

In my years in church leadership, both as a lay person and pastor, I've had countless conversations with people who say they dropped out of church because they just never felt accepted: "I felt like I was an outsider." And while I agree that there are many ways congregations can subtly exclude people, there's also a degree to which the individual has the responsibility to stop running bandit.

In his letter to the church at Corinth, the apostle Paul goes to great lengths to communicate just how vital and necessary every member is: "The eye cannot say to the hand, 'I have no need of you,' nor again the head to the feet, 'I have no need of you.' On the contrary, the members of the body that seem to be weaker are indispensable" (1 Cor. 12:21-22).

I suspect that many believers go about "churching" the same way I went about running: believing in it, enjoying it, working at it, yet holding back for fear that their talents aren't really valuable. And then feeling frustrated and lonely because they don't feel a part of the group.

Once I stopped running bandit, I still didn't win. I still didn't place. And I still didn't set any records. But I also no longer felt like an outsider. You know what else I discovered? Some of the best runners (i.e., those who did win, place, and set records) were the ones who gave me the most encouragement.

So if you feel you're on the outside looking in, examine yourself and see if maybe part of the problem is that you've been trying to run bandit.

DINNER FOR TWO

My six-year-old son wanted to know why my dinner was different from his.

"I'm trying to lose some weight, honey."

"Why do you want to lose weight?"

"Because I'm too fat." Mistake, mistake! I know better than to put myself down to my child. It's lousy role modeling.

"MOMMY! You're NOT fat!"

Good...an opportunity to redeem myself. "You're right, sweetheart, I'm not fat. I'm just not as thin as I'd like to be."

"How thin would you like to be?"

"W-e-l-l...thinner than I am."

"HOW thin?"

Don't they ever quit? "I don't know...like the movie stars, I guess."

"But Mommy, you're not a movie star."

That's right. I forgot.

Spend some time grazing through prime time television and you can see that our contemporary culture is obsessed with physical perfection. It seems to be just one more way in which people alienated from God turn to worshiping the created rather than the Creator. I wish I could hold someone responsible for poisoning our perceptions about what is and is not pleasing to the eye. But the truth is, I don't know who wrote the current book on beauty...I don't know who changed the rules on body shapes and sizes...I don't know who's marketing the "product." And perhaps most distressing, I don't know why we buy it. But I do know the kind of pain and damage that results when one attempts to conform to such artificial standards.

I've nearly cried listening to too many healthy third graders fret about being fat. I've felt my heart wrench as too many size 7 teenagers insisted they needed to diet. I've agonized with too many attractive young women who were self-destructing through bulimic behavior. And I've seen too many young men sweat out (literally) the driving compulsion to distort their physiques into a mold some magazine has deemed ideal.

Don't misunderstand me. It is important to take care of ourselves physically; it is a natural extension of a positive self-image. And we certainly cannot glorify God in our bodies if we don't do some maintenance on the "temple."

But when all efforts towards self-care and improvement are cosmetic—when it becomes excessive and obsessive—there evolves an imbalance that sets the stage for collapse, in much the same way that the shell of a building will crumble if there is nothing inside to hold it together.

As with other life struggles, the wisdom of Reinhold Neibur's "Serenity Prayer" provides help for this issue as well: Work towards accepting what you cannot change about your body. Strip down to your skivvies, stand in front of your bedroom mirror, and recite Psalm 139:14a: "I praise you, for I am fearfully and wonderfully made."

Last January, while out jogging on one of those awful, icy mornings, I encountered a working man who looked to be about three decades my senior. Taking note of my precarious, ponderous, navigation across the crusty, crunchy snow, he gave me a grizzled grin and asked, "Is that really necessary?"

Good question, my friend. Good question indeed.

My son's logic is absolutely impeccable. Those of us who are not movie stars are not required to look like them.

What a relief!

PEOPLE DISCLAIMERS

At the risk of sounding like a mother, I have to say that the fashion philosophy today leaves me a little bewildered: What's old is new, what's wrong-side out is in, what's bleached is hot, and what's torn is cool.

The people who market these things are no dummies. They know that value-minded shoppers take one look at torn, faded garments on the rack with premium price tags and say: "Seventy-five dollars for *that*? No way! It looks like somebody ruined it in the wash and returned it!" So they include a plausible disclaimer, like this one off my son's new jeans: "Uneven wash is a specialized process which is exclusive to pigment shades. The irregularities are part of the desired look, creating an individual and personal garment."

So we fall for it saying, "Oh, I get it. It's *supposed* to look that way." And voilà! Imperfections are now a status symbol.

I wish people came with such disclaimers: "The baldness trait in the Monroe men creates a smooth sheen on a head designed for thinking. Extraneous hair would be an unwelcome distraction."

"Hefty thighs are the trademark of the Watson women. The additional packaging on this woman is part of a carefully cultivated image and broadens the impact of her appeal."

"The large nose you see on the attached person is a family heirloom that has been handed down from generation to generation. It adds dimension to a face otherwise monotonous with unbroken regularity."

"The fact that the men and women in this age group wear some of their years around their middles is a trademark of Latter Days Designs. The deviation of shape is intended to create a full-bodied appeal."

I think Michael Jackson is one of the most pathetic human beings alive. For all his undeniable talent, for all his fame, for all his fortune, he obviously could not come to grips with what he considered to be his physical imperfections. I've lost track of how many cosmetic surgeries he's undergone to alter his appearance. In the early '80s he was drop-dead gorgeous. Now he has the surrealistic look of a mannequin.

On the other hand, I applaud Wal-Mart Corporation for using their employees and families in their advertisements to display merchandise. I don't know about you, but I like opening the newspaper to see models who look like people instead of some adolescent's fantasy-come-to-life.

With a little clever marketing that precipitates a change of perspective, imperfections in today's top brand name clothing are elevated from flaws to fashion statements.

So it would stand to reason that if we would be willing to change our perspective regarding the physical appearance of our fellow human beings, "imperfections" would cease to be a source of shame and rejection, and could be embraced for the spice of life that variety brings.

Maybe what I'm proposing is a bit ambitious and unrealistic. But if it's working for Tommy, Old Navy, Guess, Bugle Boy, and Wal-Mart, why not real people as well?

POTLUCKS

I've been to a lot of potlucks in my time. I come from a long line of Baptists, and my family was bent in such a way that our entire social life revolved around church functions. Christians are indeed a peculiar people. Since we tend to be conservative in lifestyle and restrained in expression, we would never consider gathering together for drunken carousing, wild orgies, or other forms of riotous living. Such temperance, however, seldom carries over into our eating habits. We *like* our food!

Yes, I know all about potlucks. And when I was a young newlywed I would take advantage of such occasions to experiment with the culinary arts.

Which was not a smart move, because it is not my nature to fuss. So after investing time and energy fussing over a dish designed to impress, I'd arrive at the event too drained and uptight to enjoy myself. Then, more than once, whatever delectable masterpiece I'd contributed was left virtually undisturbed due to the fact there were too many others who had done likewise, which created a massive surplus of food. Talk about sins of excess!

Therefore, I have learned from my experience.

I still do potlucks. And I still bring a generous amount of something delicious. The difference is, I no longer choose what I take based on what I think others might like. In fact, I give very little thought to what might please someone else. I take what I like, since I know there's a better than even chance most of it will be going home with me and I'll be the one eating it over the next several days.

I see a lot of similarities here in how we go about carving out our identities and establishing our places in the world. For too many years and through too many tears you may have found yourself forever trying to second-guess who and what others might want you to be, spent all your love and energy trying to conform to that elusive standard, and then felt bitterly disappointed when you realized you were stuck with the leftovers—a "you" you neither knew nor liked.

Several years ago Rick Nelson recorded a song whose hook line was: "Well, it's all right now, I learned my lesson well. ...You can't please everyone, so you've got to please yourself." Now, I will not give unqualified endorsement to that philosophy because for the Christian there are legitimate times and places for self-sacrifice. But the song underscores a crucial point: Sacrifice for the sake of people-pleasing is a weak counterfeit for service, and it profits no one. Let me go back to potlucks...

If I receive a specific request, I'll cooperate with it. If I'm told to bring a main dish, I'll make lasagna or a chicken casserole. If I'm assigned a salad, it'll be pasta or broccoli. And if the need is for a dessert, I'll whip up a cheesecake or something chocolate...all within the guidelines, but still things that I like and that I'll enjoy should no one else be interested.

I have no desire to feed into the narcissistic self-centeredness of our current culture. We have behavioral boundaries in life, and I want to affirm that loud and clear against the backwash of an age of relativism and situational ethics. We have legal boundaries, we have moral boundaries, we have biblical boundaries. And it is not okay to transgress such boundaries. It is sin.

But, within these boundaries we have tremendous freedom and flexibility to make choices. So we will be happier and healthier being who we want to be rather than trying to be who we think someone else wants us to be.

When you go to a potluck, be sure to take along something you like since you'll probably be the one stuck eating it. Likewise, when it comes to issues of personality and iden-

tity, make sure your outward expressions accurately reflect
your true self.

After all, you're the one who has to live with yourself.

The Ladder

One bright summer day when my son, Jameson, was five years old he locked us out of the house. Of course he didn't mean to. And of course I knew that. All the same it took a few minutes for me to move through the emotional ventilation stage and into the problem solving stage. I comforted my anxious child and told him Mommy wasn't upset anymore and she'd fix everything.

My husband wasn't due home for several hours, and the thought of spending the entire afternoon and a goodly portion of the evening in my backyard with no access to life's amenities (like the phone, refrigerator, and bathroom) didn't appeal to me at all. I was determined to find a way into my house.

The key we had hidden outside three years prior for just such an emergency must have been biodegradable since it was nowhere to be found. So Jamey and I circled our house, checking every door and window on the outside chance I'd been negligent enough to have left one unlocked. No such luck—the price we pay for efficiency!

About now you're probably thinking: Why didn't she just go somewhere and call her husband?

Excellent question...and don't think I didn't think of it! However, the operative word in that suggestion is "go." You see, I was dressed in sunbathing attire. And I simply didn't relish the thought of *going* anywhere in my almost altogether!

So as I saw it, I had one option and that was to find a way into my house even if it meant doing damage. Now, I knew that I could probably coax the attic window open. All I needed was a ladder to get up to the second story. There are times when being married to a handyman comes in handy, for there against the fence I saw not one, but three ladders...three heavy, rickety, wooden extension ladders.

Undaunted and humming the *Indiana Jones* theme song under my breath, I lugged one of the ladders across the yard and managed to situate it against the house. I was home free. All I had to do was climb up and crawl in.

And guess what I remembered about myself on the way up? I'm acrophobic, i.e., scared of heights. As I neared the top of the ladder I felt like I was enacting a scene from Hitchcock's *Vertigo*. I climbed down, said a prayer, and tried again. This time I had vivid images flashing through my mind of the ladder and me careening backwards and crashing to the ground, crushing my son beneath me and leaving us both critically injured and unconscious with the dog howling and licking our wounds.

I climbed back down.

Now, I can't claim many virtues, but I'm nothing if not tenacious, so I went back up that ladder. I waited several long minutes with a death grip on the frame, mentally sizing up the distance between myself and the window. Two and a half, maybe three feet at the most. And since a disproportionate length of my sixty-six inches is located in my legs, it should have been a simple matter to stretch across the abyss and step in.

So I told myself.

Anchoring my left foot firmly on the rung, I tentatively ventured out with my right foot...and felt the ladder slide. With knees of Jell-O and arms of spaghetti, I wobbled back down.

I couldn't do it. I had the will and I had the way, but I couldn't implement my solution.

About that time I sensed rather than heard my neighbor in his own backyard. Why I didn't think of it sooner I can't tell you, but like a proselyte quickening to the call I arose, approached him, and said, "I have a problem. Would you help me?"

This time it was a cinch. With my neighbor steadying the ladder, I scrambled up, grabbed hold, pushed off, and pulled myself inside. Mission accomplished.

No matter how smart, no matter how strong, no matter how self-sufficient, no matter how spiritual you may be, sometimes you've just got to ask for help. You may have identified your problem. You even may have arrived at a workable solution. But more often than not you need someone else to stabilize and support you in order to turn your plan into action.

Makes a lot of sense, doesn't it? And you probably think that it's somehow easier to put into practice for those of us who make a living and a mission out of helping others.

Don't you believe it for a minute.

NUTTIN' FOR CHRISTMAS

Studies have shown that snooping is a learned behavior. I know for a fact that is true, because I learned it from my brother.

December 1963...Aunt Mary's house:

I was eight, he was nine. Mark called me back into the spare bedroom (the one that was cold because the registers were closed, and clean because the kids weren't allowed in there). He was stretched out on his belly peering under the bed: "Robin, look...Christmas presents!" I scooted down beside him, and there, sure enough, were bags full of colorful things.

Being something of an evangelist even then, I carried the good news to my five-year-old cousin: "Look Karen...Christmas presents!" I don't know where Mark disappeared to (he always left me holding the bag), but the next thing I remember is walking into the kitchen, and there's my dear, adorable little cousin *telling her mother* about our discovery.

Now, to get the full impact of this, you need to understand Karen. Her long dark hair was always in ringlets or braids. She wore saddle shoes and sailor suits. She never lied, argued, sassed, disobeyed, or got dirty. Being a perfect child, she had no concept that there are just *some* things parents don't *need* to know.

And there's my Aunt Mary—my favorite aunt, the only grown-up I knew who chewed bubble gum, allowed the dog on the furniture, and got her hair wet when we went swimming—giving me "the look" while saying to her daughter, "No sweetheart, those presents aren't for you. *Santa* brings the presents on Christmas Eve. But [and her tone takes on an unmistakable pointedness] he only brings them to *good* little boys and girls."

"He's making a list, checking it twice, gonna find out who's naughty and nice..."

I was mortified. I was terrified. I was petrified!

Christmas Eve was a restless night for me. I awoke while

it was still pitch-black outside. Then—with much fear and trembling—I sneaked out to the Christmas tree, only to see that my worse fears had come true: nothing.

Devastated, I raced back to my bottom bunk and began a litany of prayers and promises. Hours passed. Or maybe it was minutes. The gray light of dawn began to lift the shadows. So, holding my breath and holding back tears, I inched back out to the living room.

If I could put this on film for you, you would see a little girl in red sleepers, short, brown hair, and large dark eyes that slowly (as the camera zooms in for a close up) get larger while the stringed background music swells to crescendo with the words:

> *Grace, grace, God's grace...*
> *Grace that is greater than all my sin,*
> *Grace that is greater than all my sin.**

It was all there...the filled stockings, the Chatty Baby doll in her highchair, Koko the stuffed Orangutan. It was all there all the time. I was just too blinded by my guilt to see the gifts.

Too many of us year after year approach Christmas the same way—with raw memories of recent mistakes and fresh failures. We know we have been naughty and not nice. Right or wrong, we are too blinded by our guilt to see the Gift.

But the good news of the gospel is that God is bigger, and better, and more generous than Santa could ever hope to be: "When the fullness of time had come, God sent his Son, born of a woman, born under the law" (Gal. 4:4). And "God proves his love for us in that while we still were sinners Christ died for us" (Rom. 5:8).

God's gift of grace in Jesus is not just for the good little boys and girls. "While we still were *sinners*"—while we were still naughty and not nice—Christ *came*.

"Thanks be to God for his indescribable gift!" (2 Cor. 9:15).

*Julia H. Johnston, 1911

SECOND CHOICE, SECOND CHANCE

I've been transcribing information from my old address book into a new one—a project that has generated a kaleidoscope of memories and emotions as I weed out names. I smiled with fondness at the names of previous coworkers. I sighed in resignation at the names of probation kids I supervised. I sniffled with nostalgic longing for the names of college and seminary friends. And then I shuddered, feeling a fresh wave of grief at the names connected with the App clan…the names that are no longer family to me.

I could have sworn hell would freeze over before I'd ever wind up divorced. If someone had told me on July 16, 1977, that fourteen years later my pastor husband would walk away from the marriage and values he once held sacred, I would not have even flinched. I'd have laughed aloud, so sure, so secure, so elated were we that day.

The Twilight Zone of divorce has been a grueling nightmare of disillusionment, depression, and despair for me. I lost sleep; I lost weight; I lost perspective; I lost control; and I nearly lost my mind. But praise God I didn't lose friends, and thanks to them I didn't lose faith.

I've asked a thousand unanswered whys and have cried enough tears to fill a baptistery. During this dark night I picked up a little book with an irresistible title: *Lord, Don't You Love Me Anymore?* In it, Ruth Harms Calkin prays: "O God, teach me well…teach me well. It is drastically important that the pain of this past year is not wasted. How tragic it would be to suffer so much and gain so little…teach me well, O God."

What have I learned? A lot. But two elementary principles stand out:

1. Prayer has less to do with getting what we want out of God, than with surrendering what we want to God.

2. The Christian life is not about finding happiness, but about practicing faithfulness.

For each name that did not get recorded in my new address book, I said a prayer that it would indeed be recorded in heaven where there will be no more brokenness and no more good-byes. While the project itself has been an emotional mix, the reason for it is pure joy, for the new book is filling up as I address wedding invitations. God has blessed me with a dream-come-true relationship in the form of a tall, blond, blue-eyed German with a big heart, a sensitive spirit, and an uncompromising faith. He is secure enough not to be intimidated by me, smart enough not to be manipulated by me, good-humored enough to joke about his role as a pastor's "wife," and romantic enough to propose to me (on one knee yet) in front of my congregation one Sunday morning.

So not only do I have a new address book, I'll have a new name and a whole new set of family and friends to record in it. Yet, even in the midst of our rejoicing there is ongoing pain, for the fallout from divorce never ends. Just ask our six boys.

My soon-to-be-husband and I both believe that God's *first* choice would have been to heal the marriages of our youth. The fact, however, that neither of us chose to default on those covenants helps lay the foundation of trust and respect for our new covenant.

New address book, new name, new family, new home, new start. The amazing part of God's amazing grace is that second choice does not have to mean second best, but instead can mean second chance.

II | WHEN YOU'VE WANDERED FROM THE PATH OF RIGHTEOUSNESS...

Learning from mistakes

TOP BUNK INITIATION

There's a photograph my mother has of me and three of my brothers that was taken at Christmastime. The brothers are all wearing red corduroy pants and white dress shirts, while I have on a red velvet skirt and a white frilly blouse. We are posed in front of my mom's S&H Green Stamps bookcase which had been cleverly disguised as a snow-capped chimney. I must say we were adorable. But you don't have to look too closely to notice that in addition to my seasonal attire and big smile, I am also wearing two black eyes.

Those black eyes were my souvenir from a few days previously when my older brother Mark told me that since my name was Robin I could fly and challenged me to do so off our top bunk. Truly, I don't even remember the incident (perhaps the bump on my forehead caused selective amnesia?). I know the story only from the evidence of pictures and the testimony of family legend.

I don't recall if Mark was punished in any way for setting me up as he did. It was a mean trick to be sure, but it was also the kind of thing that big brothers have been doing to little sisters since the dawn of time. In retrospect, I'm kind of proud of him.

My black eyes resulted from a combination of Mark's manipulation and my gullibility. Which is to say that none of our experiences happen in a vacuum. They are invariably the product of others' influence and our choices. Sometimes we make smart choices. And sometimes we don't. But regardless of whether our initial choice is right or wrong, good or bad, healthy or un, it is always redeemable when we learn from it. That certainly was not the last time Mark manipulated me. But I am proud to say that nearly forty years have passed, and I have never again attempted to fly off a top bunk!

THE PRODIGAL DOG

My dog just did a night in The Joint.

It all began on a summer's day not unlike others. The adults went to work, the kids went to the sitter's, and Yogi went to the backyard. Confined by the fence, equipped with shelter, and provided with water, there was no reason to worry.

Except for the gate.

Now, to date no one has admitted to leaving it open. And we have no idea how long Yogi contented himself with the limited pleasantries of his own backyard before he noticed his opportunity for escape. But at some point he obviously did notice, and made a break for freedom.

What a wide wonderful world it must've seemed! So much new territory to claim, so many trails to investigate, so many butterflies to chase, so many intruders to intimidate, so many delicious aromas wafting in from the east....

Food, his little doggie brain registered. *Better yet, people food! Lets just find out where it's coming from.* I can just see him with visions of French fries dancing in his head, trotting towards the source.

The problem was, however, that between Yogi and his destination lay four lanes of heavily trafficked highway. A younger dog might've been more quick. A stray dog might've been more street smart. A bigger dog might've been more visible. Yogi probably never knew what hit him.

Lucky for us all there was a good Samaritan passing by who was moved with compassion for one small, shaken, and shivering fox terrier. So twenty-four hours (and at least twenty-four phone calls) later, we located him at the animal shelter.

As my husband entered the high-security section with cells full of yapping inmates, Yogi, battered and bruised, looked up at him with soulful eyes that said: "I have sinned against heaven and in your sight, and I am no longer worthy to be called your dog."

Okay, maybe I am carrying it a bit far. But I see at least three lessons for us in Yogi's ordeal:

1. *Freedom run amuck enslaves.* Second Peter 2:19 says: "They promise freedom, but they themselves are slaves of corruption; for people are slaves to whatever masters them." Freedom is indeed a glorious blessing. But it is a blessing that carries with it an awesome responsibility. Improperly exercised it can have terrifying consequences. Yogi's unrestrained pursuit of freedom ultimately brought him stricter confinement.

2. *Boundaries are for our benefit.* Whether you're a toddler living with rules about crossing the street, a teenager living with guidelines on curfews, a single adult living with standards of celibacy, or an alcoholic living with mandates of abstinence, boundaries serve the purpose of keeping us safe and healthy. That's why God tells us: "For you were called to freedom, brothers and sisters; only do not use your freedom as an opportunity for self-indulgence" (Gal. 5:13). Unfortunately, like Yogi, most of us choose to learn this the hard way.

3. *Redemption is expensive.* In order to redeem Yogi from the shelter, it cost me exactly sixteen dollars more than I paid for him as a pup. Had Yogi respected the boundaries we set for him, it would've saved us time, money, and grief. My husband's first words to the little bundle of nerves he scooped up were: "You owe me, dog!"

While Scripture assures us that God's welcoming words to his prodigals are far more compassionate than my husband's to Yogi, the sentiment is the same: "Or do you not know...that you are not your own? For you were bought with a price" (1 Cor. 6:19-20*a*).

Yogi was very fortunate to have a network of caring that brought him home. So are we.

> *Prone to wander, Lord, I feel it,*
> *Prone to leave the God I love.*
> *Here's my heart, O take and seal it,*
> *Seal it for thy courts above.*
>
>> —from "Come Thou Fount"
>> (Robert Robinson, 1758)

THE WRONG TURN

The line at the fast food restaurant was long for midafternoon. So I left my son waiting at the counter while I navigated through the seating section, rushed down the hallway, took a sharp turn to the left, burst through the door, and there on my right saw…urinals.

My very first thought was: *Now why are they putting urinals in the women's restroom?*

Maybe you haven't found yourself in the wrong restroom lately. But I'll bet there have been times you've taken a wrong turn, and your first reaction was to assume that someone else had.

Remember the bank statement you raised Cain over, only to discover later that your spouse had made an ATM withdrawal and forgotten to record it?

What about the responsibility lecture you gave your teenager on the low gas tank, only to remember that you were the last one to use the car?

Let's face it, we all like to be right. But there is a world of difference between being right and getting right. Had I been determined to be right, I would have attempted to prove that I was actually in the women's room. Someone had just mistakenly installed urinals in it!

Ridiculous? Of course it is. But some of the scenarios played out in families and organizations are equally unfounded:

An athlete quits the team because "the coach doesn't know what he's doing." The team goes on to win the championship.

A woman leaves her husband because she is so miserably unhappy. Five years later she's alone, struggling financially, and still miserably unhappy.

A congregation gets rid of a pastor because the church isn't growing. Ten years and 3.7 pastors later, the church still isn't growing. Or…

The church *is* growing. But growing in a way that disrupts the status quo. The pastor is out, tradition is in, attendance is down, and nobody talks about what really happened.

A church member objects to a proposal. When the vote goes the other way, he refuses to support the decision of the body and instead boycotts services and withholds financial support.

"Why do you see the speck in your neighbor's eye, but do not notice the log in your own eye?... You hypocrite, first take the log out of your own eye, and then you will see clearly to take the speck out of your neighbor's eye" (Matt. 7:3, 5). How quickly we agree with it...how reluctantly we practice it.

I suppose I could have gone to the manager of the restaurant and complained that the urinals were in the wrong restroom. I could have found a crowbar and pried them off the wall. I could have switched the signs on the outside of the doors. And if being right was my ultimate goal, I would have done any or all of those things.

But in that situation, getting right was a lot more important to me than being right. And the only way to get right was to admit I was wrong. I exited the men's room red-faced and grateful for the vacancy that spared me further embarrassment.

If being right is your consuming passion, it's easy enough to achieve that illusion. All you have to do is stubbornly insist that everyone else is wrong and blindly ignore all information that challenges your presuppositions. You won't fool anyone else; to others you'll be as obvious as a woman in a men's restroom. You can, however, create a nice little bubble of denial that will insulate you from the truth.

If, on the other hand, you're less interested in being right, and more interested in getting right, the straight and narrow path to that end is learning to admit when you're wrong.

And start with little things—it'll prepare you for the big ones.

GROCERY STORES AND GROWLING STOMACHS

I walked into the grocery store one day with three items on my list and a five-dollar bill in my pocket. What could be simpler?

The problem was that I'd skipped breakfast and it was almost noon. So in addition to my original three items, look what I had at the checkout: three packages of Oreos, one pound of pistachio nuts, one package of sourdough English muffins, one package of fresh bagels, one Tombstone double-top pizza, three boxes of Pop Tarts, one loaf of garlic bread, and two boxes of Little Debbie oatmeal pies!

I wish I could tell you I was fabricating this scenario, but unfortunately it's not even an exaggeration. When I wheeled up to the cashier, my five dollars was pathetically insufficient, so I had to dig for my checkbook and take from Peter to pay Paul.

Maybe you've had a similar experience. If so, you don't need me to point out that when we are physically hungry we don't make rational choices in what we eat. In the same way, when we are emotionally hungry we are much more inclined to make destructive, irrational life choices. And when it comes time to settle accounts, we find ourselves without sufficient resources to manage.

Take the dynamics of an extramarital affair, for instance. All too often an emotionally starved spouse chooses to become sexually involved with someone else. Whether it's a wife who feels neglected or a husband who feels rejected, the message is loud and clear: "I want someone to love me and appreciate me and make me feel special and important. And if you won't do it I'll find somebody who will." The method of communication (the affair) however, is so destructive with guilt, shame, and blame that the message goes virtually unnoticed.

This irrational choice born out of emotional hunger leads to pain, anger, broken trust, and possibly even the loss of a marriage. Most spouses who make this choice find themselves ill-equipped to cope with its consequences.

I see a lot of unmet emotional needs at the root of much rebellion. Many who abuse substances, engage in promiscuity, run away, drop out, get arrested, marry the wrong person, divorce the right one, or turn their backs on God are making irrational choices out of emotional deprivation. However, while the hunger is real and the need is valid, the method chosen to meet the need is counterproductive at best and, more often than not, downright destructive. The solution does nothing to solve the problem.

In my experience, Christians are notorious for ignoring their emotional hunger. Because we believe in a lifestyle of servanthood we often incorrectly translate that into total denial of our own needs. And we all know someone (or have *been* someone) who has traveled down one of the paths mentioned above, with tragic results.

Reversing the pattern requires rethinking the assumptions. Recognize that your needs are legitimate and accept responsibility for getting them met. This is not selfishness; this is stewardship. Then when making choices, consider the old adage, "Look before you leap."

If you are teetering on the brink of a decision of life-changing proportions, force yourself to think through the consequences. Keep asking, "And then what?" after considering each possible successive choice.

If you find you're answering "I don't care!" to irrational choices with damaging consequences, realize you are hurting desperately. So take a risk and talk to someone you trust. And if that confidant disappoints you, take a deep breath and trust someone else.

Ignoring emotional hunger is risky business. It's one of the ways we give sin opportunity. Sooner or later unmet needs will take their toll and demand fulfillment. Whether it will be through constructive or destructive methods pivots on the choice we make. When I walked with a growling stomach among the multitude of temptations at the grocery store, I wound up at the checkout with a carload of unhealthy choices and a shortage of funds.

If you feel your emotions growling, be very careful in shopping for affirmation.

Messing with the IRS

When I looked down at the mail and saw "Internal Revenue Service" on one of the envelopes, I felt my blood run cold. I stared at it for several seconds, dreading the contents.

Did we make a mistake? Unlikely. Our tax preparer is meticulous.

A refund, perhaps? Ha!

This is ridiculous, I thought. *We paid our taxes in full and on time.* I tore open the envelope, scanned the letter, then yelped for my husband.

"Horst! Can you believe this rip-off?!" I exclaimed, handing him the letter. "They're trying to milk us for another fifty-six dollars—and I don't want to pay it!" He took the letter, read it, and placed a call to our tax preparer. Afterwards he told me, "Karin recommends we pay it; she says they nailed her on that same clause."

I, however, wasn't about to capitulate so easily. The blood that had previously run cold was now boiling. To some people fifty-six dollars isn't worth fighting over. But our budget is a little too tight to let that amount slip away unchallenged. Besides, I felt there was a principle at stake.

"Robin," my ever-practical husband cautioned, "Karin says we can't win."

"We'll see about that!"

As if accepting the gauntlet for a duel, I snatched the IRS letter, did an about face, walked ten paces, turned, aimed...and typed. Then, almost as an afterthought, I picked up the phone and punched in the number listed for customer service. To my surprise, a real, live voice answered.

"Yes, I'm calling to object to this bill we received for fifty-six dollars..."

My assertiveness was textbook perfect: I politely expressed my complaint, articulately stated my case, and firmly declined to pay the penalty. And then something really, *really* awful happened: The IRS representative explained the billing to me *in a way that I understood it.*

Let me tell you, there's just nothing that will take the wind out of your sails more quickly than realizing you're wrong. All I had left to say was, "Oh...never mind then."

I've thought about that incident several times in the past couple of weeks. And it occurs to me that most of the conflict we experience with spouses, coworkers, family, or fellow church members could be dramatically reduced by taking the initiative to listen to the other's perspective, giving enough ground to receive what is said...and granting enough grace to concede that maybe...just maybe...the other's perspective makes more sense. This time.

I still don't like the IRS regulation that set me up for another fifty-six dollars. And I plan to vote for the first representative who pledges to get it changed! But I do thank God for the periodic frustrations that can teach (even those of us who learn the hard way) more about what it means to "lead a life worthy of the calling to which [we] have been called, with all humility and gentleness, with patience, bearing with one another in love, making every effort to maintain the unity of the Spirit in the bond of peace" (Eph. 4:1-3).

A TALE OF TWO TWINKIES

Whenever I have Twinkies, I always eat two.

Back when Twinkies were only available in dual pack-ages, my mother would buy two packages for my three brothers and me to share, rationing each of us to one apiece.

There came a summer when I was off to day camp, which of course meant a sack lunch. Wonder of wonders, as a rare treat my mother included an undivided package of Twinkies all for me. I was elated. Visions of sponge cake and creme filling danced in my head on the bus trip to the camp.

After we arrived at the park, my friend Glynda approached me and began discussing lunch: "I have a baloney sandwich. What do you have? Do you have milk or Kool-aid? My mom packed me an apple, but no dessert and I really wanted dessert. I can't believe she didn't pack me any dessert. Did your mom send you dessert?"

"Why yes," I said proudly, "I have two Twinkies."

"Really!?" I didn't catch on to her excitement until it was too late. "Then you can give one to me."

I'd waited a long time for this bountiful fare and had no desire to share my precious Twinkies. Since I was totally taken aback, I did what most people do in such situations: I made no commitment and attempted to avoid her.

Which didn't work. Glynda attached herself to me like a barnacle all the while maintaining a running commentary with others about lunch: "My mom didn't even pack dessert for me but I may [significant look in my direction] get some."

When lunchtime came, naturally Glynda was right beside me watching my every bite. "Are you going to give me one of your Twinkies?" I opened the package of Twinkies and silently ate the first one while Glynda accelerated her campaign: "You're almost done. Are you going to give me the other one, huh, are you? I didn't get any dessert and I'm really hungry for dessert…"

Finally, I took the second Twinkie, broke it in two, and gave her half. I still remember the twin emotions of guilt over not sharing equally, and resentment over having to share at all.

"Whoever has two coats must share with anyone who has none; and whoever has food must do likewise" (Luke 3:11). I know that now. I knew it then. The point is, though, that our perceived needs, and consequently our perceived deprivations, affect our choices about sharing.

Now, it's not like I'm going to start a recovery group for ADTKs (Adults Deprived of Twinkies as Kids). But, for instance, if I'd believed there would soon be another two-Twinkle lunch, I might've shared more graciously. If Glynda had believed her mother would send dessert the next day, she might've waited more patiently.

There's no escaping the fact, however, that giving ultimately involves sacrifice. And right or wrong, our ability to sacrifice is intricately connected to those perceived deprivations.

Many of you, when challenged by your churches to give, do exactly what I did with

Glynda: commit to nothing and avoid situations where you're reminded of the request. Then, when you feel cornered, you grudgingly give about half of what you could give. Which in turn leaves you feeling guilty and resentful. No fun, huh?

There's a better way.

When you consider what God would have you give, don't think in terms of dollars. Think in terms of deprivations felt over unmet needs. Because giving is really not about financial planning at all. It's about spiritual regeneration.

As you review those unmet needs, surrender them to God. Then you'll find that one of two things will happen: God will either meet the unmet need, or God will heal the distorted perception. Once you experience that, sharing becomes as natural and easy as...well, eating.

REBOUNDS AND REDEMPTION

Sports analogies usually get me in trouble. I don't have a competitive bone in my body, so I can't relate to the mentality that approaches each game with the holy zeal of a crusade.

Having said that, however, I am, after all, a Hoosier. And whether it's in the water or in the blood, it's impossible to grow up in Indiana without developing some affinity for basketball.

I'm a Pacer fan. Now, I don't paint my face blue and gold. I don't memorize the stats of games and players. And I haven't actually seen a game live since my church youth group used to go watch Mel Daniels, George McGinnis, and Billy Keller play in the old Coliseum with the ABA's red, white, and blue basketball. *Fan* is a relative term. By using it to describe myself I mean that if the Pacers are playing, I would never root against them.

So naturally, during game seven of the 1998 NBA playoffs I was hoping to see the Pacers defeat the Bulls and win their first Eastern Conference championship.

It didn't happen.

And while I didn't feel a need to put on sackcloth and ashes, I was invested enough to follow some of the postgame analysis—which revealed something very, very interesting. The final score said that the Chicago Bulls won that game by five points. But the statistics revealed that they actually won the game on the strength of their offensive rebounds: twenty-two to the Pacer's five.

What's that got to do with redemption? Just this: No matter how badly we want something, no matter how skilled we may be, no matter how sincere our efforts, no matter how straight we may shoot, there will be times when we miss.

On a personal level, when our vocabulary slips, that's a miss. When our patience snaps, that's a miss. When our morals collapse, that's a miss. When greed, sloth, or envy prevail, that's a miss.

I know that as a pastor, when church attendance drops, it feels like a miss to me. When offerings dip, it feels like a miss. When visitors don't return, or newcomers fizzle, or members fade away, it feels like a miss to me.

Sin literally means "to miss the mark." So for each of us, anytime we blow it or anytime we try but don't get the results we wanted, it feels like a miss.

But if we can learn anything from championship basketball teams it is this: Even when we miss we can still gain victory—as long as we follow through with the rebound and keep trying.

"Therefore, my beloved, be steadfast, immovable, always excelling in the work of the Lord, because you know that your labor is not in vain" (1 Cor. 15:58).

Striking the Rock

It wasn't a terminal mistake. It wasn't an expensive mistake. It wasn't an unredeemable mistake. It's just that it was, and remains, an embarrassing mistake.

It happened several years ago. My first husband had just filed for divorce. Soon after, I received another shock upon learning there were several thousand dollars of debt. Needless to say, my emotional health was not at its best.

There was an angry confrontation over the debt with a lot of mutual blaming. After several minutes of this chaotic communication, I did something I had never done before, have never done since, and with God's help will never do again: I hit him. Really. With all the frustration, venom, and irrationality of Moses striking the rock, I raised my hand and struck him. Once.

Chances are, some of you are chuckling...perhaps because you understand. But friends, violence is not a laughing matter. Nobody chuckles when a man hits his estranged wife.

I don't think there's anything I've done in my life of which I am more ashamed. So why am I telling you? Because I learned something from it and I think you can too.

First of all, for those of you who have never done such a thing, have never contemplated doing such a thing, and are aghast that someone could do such a thing—please bear in mind that people going through major crises and losses can get a little crazy and do things they'd never do in less stressful circumstances. We're no longer allowed to use the term diagnostically, but the phrase *temporary insanity* has descriptive value here.

I don't think it's coincidence that ten verses prior to Moses's violent outburst in Numbers 20:11, his sister Miriam had died and was buried. Grief and loss often generate and exacerbate anger.

Secondly, for those of you who are prone to acting out your anger in destructive ways, you need to know this. I didn't phase my ex-husband; I didn't hurt him and I didn't change him. I did, however, break my hand.

It was awful. I delayed going to the doctor for two weeks because I knew he'd ask how it had happened. Finally, when I couldn't take the pain and could no longer deny the fact, I went for an x-ray.

He was so excited: "Look here, Robin, it's broken all right. See that little chip of bone? It's what we call a boxer's fracture."

Thanks, Doc, I needed that.

"What'd you do," he chuckled, "get mad and hit a wall?"

"Something like that." (It was true, metaphorically speaking.)

I wore a splint for several weeks, fielded a lot of questions, and to this day feel an occasional twinge of pain in my right hand.

So here's the moral to the story: Destructive anger has a boomerang effect. This holds true whether it be vitriolic words that diminish credibility, passive-aggressive behavior that results in isolation, grudges that poison spirits, or betrayal that damages trust.

When we act out anger destructively, not only is it not effective—not only is it sin—we ultimately wind up hurting ourselves as much, if not more than, we hurt anyone or anything else.

God forgave me immediately when I confessed. My ex forgave me the next day when I apologized. It took a little longer for me to forgive myself.

I hope my story will help you to make wiser, healthier choices when consumed with anger during your own crisis.

The Disconnection

My phone was disconnected recently. And all because I hadn't paid my bill.

Picky, picky, picky.

Now there were reasons I hadn't paid it. Good reasons. The phone company, however, was not impressed with my reasons. Their narrow-minded, legalistic logic was: No money, no service.

Naturally, during the twenty-four hours it was disconnected I had an influx of calls. So, heaped upon my frustration was the professional embarrassment of my clients (you know, the people who pay me to help them learn to better manage their lives?) receiving a recording informing them in so many words that their counselor apparently doesn't know how to keep her own house in order!

Then, adding injury to insult, I learn I'll have to pay a reconnect fee.

We are daily presented with series of interlocking choices to make, and in one way or another, whether we like it or not, we're accountable for those choices.

Sometimes we make a choice and later realize that its consequences were harmful or detrimental in some way. Upon reflection we sincerely regret the choice and wish we had made a different one.

We call these "mistakes."

Hopefully then we examine that choice and its results and notice what went wrong and what we could have done differently and what we need to do the next time. Then, if we remember wisely and well, we do better when presented with similar options.

We call this "learning."

So we benefit from the experience and admit our error and accept its consequences, realizing that little good will result from either scapegoating or self-recrimination.

We call this "maturity."

Other times we inherit the consequences or get caught in the crossfire of others' choices which may not be in our best interests, and we wind up suffering for something we did not cause and do not deserve.

We call this "life."

At which point we take a deep breath, say a prayer and continue on, reminding ourselves that the magic lens of retrospect will eventually reassure us that somehow, someday, some way we'll be able to believe such things work together for the good.

We call this "faith."

Maybe it's simplistic to point out that life isn't fair. But it isn't. At the same time that is not to say we should accept everything that's handed to us or that we should never fight. There are many times when it is in everyone's best interests to hold another accountable for his or her choices. And I'll never encourage anyone to live as a victim.

It's just that there are also times when we want to fight and there's really no enemy...times when we want to blame and it's no one's fault...times when we'd like to flee and there's no escape. And it is in just such times that the only viable option is to adapt...to go with the flow...to roll with the punches...to make lemonade out of lemons.

I haven't surrendered yet on the reconnect fee for my phone. I doubt however that I'll win this one, and I expect I'll end up paying the penalty for my oversight.

Maybe I can write it off as "tuition."

Set in Concrete

The day the contractors came to pour our new driveway my young son and I watched in fascination as the wet concrete flowed down the chute of the giant mixer like gray cake batter, then as the workers spread, coaxed, and nursed it to smooth perfection.

As I went in and out of the house checking the driveway's progress I had to restrain Yogi, our miniature fox terrier, who wanted so badly to be out where all the action was. But dogs can't stay inside forever; they have business outdoors. So eventually I escorted him into the backyard to answer nature's call.

To this day I don't know how it happened. I thought I'd been careful to seal off all avenues of escape. But as Yogi and I reentered the house our eyes simultaneously landed on the wide-open door leading out to the freshly finished driveway. Yogi's ears perked up in delight while my jaw dropped in dismay. If this were a movie, the next few seconds would be in slow motion...

I lunged for the dog, who neatly slipped out of my grasp, easily outmaneuvered my clumsy groping, and rocketed towards the wet cement in the wake of my "No, Yogi! No, no, no, NO, *NO!*"

Yogi never broke stride. He glanced once over his shoulder, and if a dog could thumb his nose I'm sure he would have. I watched in frozen horror as he did the very thing I'd tried all day to prevent, leaving on the glass-like surface of the virgin concrete little puppy paw prints that I feared were embedded into eternity.

The face of the worker who'd been posted sentry was totally expressionless. Chagrined at having been out-foxed by a fox terrier, I choked out, "Is it too late to fix that?" Without a word he picked up his trowel and ambled towards the damage.

I located my four-legged fugitive, who was happily bark-
ing his head off at two nervous little girls. Scooping him up,
I delivered a scathing diatribe denouncing canine intelligence
in general while Yogi gazed adoringly up at me as if to say,
"Gee, you're beautiful when you're angry!" As I turned
towards home I dreaded the sight of my driveway. But as we
approached the house, I was amazed to see the last traces of
his transgression being neatly smoothed away.

In our modern vernacular, we use the phrase "set in concrete" to describe that which cannot be changed. But as I
gazed upon my regenerated driveway I could almost hear a
scriptural medley of newness singing through my spirit: "I am
making all things *new*...anyone in Christ is a *new* creature...put on the *new* self...walk in the *newness* of life...hope
upon hope of *new* songs...*new* wine...*new* garments...*new*
names...*new* tongues...*new* covenants...*new* heavens...and
new Earth."

Even now as I write, my mind is flooded with a montage
of faces—wounded people scarred and marred by sin and
suffering whose lives are being metamorphosed by the trans-
forming grace of God. Some are courageously reconstructing
the fallout of their own choices; others creatively coping with
the uninvited, undeserved damage inflicted upon them. All
triumphantly new.

It's funny how ordinary places become holy. My driveway
forever reminds me that no matter how devastating the damage, how deep the pain, or how great the guilt, there is
always hope for healing.

Even when something's been set in concrete.

III | WHEN YOU'VE FALLEN AND CAN'T GET UP...
Growing through painful experiences

OF PEARLS AND PAIN

I'm not much of one for baubles, bangles, and beads. Most of my costume jewelry has long since found its way to the church rummage sale. And it would take only one hand to count the number of so-called real pieces tucked away in my boudoir. In spite of that, I've always felt an emotional bond with pearls. Once I discovered how they're formed, I realized why.

The pearl is the only gem made by a living process. It starts with the accidental entry of foreign matter into the oyster. The poor little guy does not ask for this problem; it neither expects nor deserves it. Once the irritant is a part of the oyster's life, however, it is there to stay. And the oyster spends the rest of its living days attempting to cope with it.

It does this by covering the irritant with a nacreous substance consisting primarily of calcium carbonate. Nothing rich or fancy—just the same healing compound used in over-the-counter antacids. The pearl evolves as concentric layers of the soothing substance form around the irritant. The oyster is a persistent little creature. Day after day...layer upon layer...hope upon hope—it never ceases its efforts to cope with pain.

More often than not, the irritant is organic rather than mineral, which means it eventually disintegrates, leaving no clue as to what initiated the oyster's coping strategy. We know how the process works. We know that it is arduous and painful. We know that the end result is something breathtakingly beautiful. We just don't always know *why*.

The irony is incredible. For centuries kings and shamans have revered the pearl for its mysterious powers and esoteric beauty. To the little oyster though, the pearl is simply a by-product of doing the best it can, with what it has, to cope with pain.

When we hurt and we don't understand why...when we've fallen and can't get up...when problems invade our lives and refuse to go away...it helps to remember that we may have a pearl in process.

SMILEY FACE THEOLOGY

I said I'd never do it. I said it looked terminally boring. I said it was an activity that promoted narcissism, not fitness. I said I preferred the open roads of jogging to the sweatshops of weight training.

In spite of all that I said, I joined a fitness center awhile back, hoping that an exercise routine which required neither daylight nor decent weather would better accommodate my schedule. And I must say that after three months of working with weights, I still prefer jogging!

There's a particular weight machine called the Rotary Torture...I mean the Rotary Torso. To use it, you sit down, grasp the handle, keep your arms and bottom half stationary while you use your inner and outer oblique muscles (that's "midriff bulge" in layman's terms) to move the handle from side to side as far as possible.

Now, when this is done properly, the upper half of your body moves in a steady sweep of almost one hundred eighty degrees. This means that if you don't keep your eyes focused on a fixed spot, you'll get dizzy and light-headed from a room that appears to be swirling by. The logical thing to look at is the bar right in front of your face since it moves with you.

Well, some joker long ago decided to stick a smiley face on that bar. Maybe to you that sounds like a nice touch. But for someone sweating and struggling through several dozen grueling repetitions, a smiley face seems to mock rather than encourage.

If I were to name one mistake that more Christians make more often than any other mistake, it is responding to the pain of others with smiley face theology:

"Your mother died? Cheer up, she's with the Lord now."

"You had a miscarriage? Well, at least you're young enough to have another baby."

"You didn't get the job? Just remember that when God closes a door he opens a window."

"Your husband has cancer? You know God doesn't give us anything we can't handle."

"Your ex just got married? There'll be someone for you too."

"Your son's been arrested? Don't forget that all things work together for the good of those who love God."

I like the Living Bible's paraphrase of Proverbs 25:20: "Being happy-go-lucky around a person whose heart is heavy is as bad as stealing his jacket in cold weather, or rubbing salt in his wounds."

Just yesterday I spoke with a dear sister in my congregation who has had more surgeries and debilitating complications in the last fifteen years than most people would have in fifteen lifetimes. She'd just returned from the doctor who, predictably, had found something else wrong. As she talked, I listened. So deep is her pain, so unrelenting is her suffering, that I knew no words adequate to alleviate them. After a few minutes she thanked me, said she always felt better after talking to me, and hung up.

It is very important to underscore that I said absolutely nothing of any consequence to her. I bestowed no words of wisdom; I applied no clinical expertise; I quoted no Scripture; I gave no advice; I offered no solutions. I just listened.

When people are suffering, smiley face theology makes a mockery of their pain. They do not need someone trying to solve their problems or cheer them up. They just need someone to listen and acknowledge that their problems are real and their pain is valid.

A few days ago at the gym I sat down and the Rotary Torso and realized that apparently I have a kindred spirit; that smiley face had been ripped off.

Which made *me* smile.

HUMPTY DUMPTY

Humpty Dumpty sat on a wall,
Humpty Dumpty had a great fall,
All the king's horses and all the king's men
Couldn't put Humpty together again.

I don't know the historical reason why Humpty Dumpty is always pictured as an egg, but I understand the symbolic significance. What could be more precarious than an egg on a wall? And what could be more fragile than fractured trust?

Trust is not inherently fragile. On the contrary, developmental psychologists consider trust to be one of the building blocks of the personality. Erik Erikson theorized that the ability to trust was established during the first year of life. And faith, the theological brand name for trust, can be a powerful source of strength.

So trust in and of itself is not weak and delicate. But what makes trust like the proverbial egg on the wall is that it is so vulnerable to outside attacks. All too often we have absolutely no control over the damage rendered our trust. It can happen without warning, without consent, without our participation, and sometimes without our conscious knowledge.

Recently I listened to a woman who had silently borne the pain of fractured trust for nearly forty years. A professional who had never married and had no children, she was the epitome of strength and self-sufficiency. For her, it was time for the silence to be broken. The years peeled back in a torrent of words and a flood of tears. I barely made a sound for nearly an hour while I listened to one episode after another of trust betrayed. When she finished, I read the question in her eyes before she formed it with her lips: "What about you? Can I trust you?" I felt as if I had been handed the Holy Grail, so sacred was the moment.

Those we love have the greatest power to fracture our trust. For example, if my waitress promises to be right back with more coffee and she doesn't come, I feel annoyed. But if my dad promises to come to my ball game and never shows, I feel abandoned.

If my college sweetheart breaks up with me for another, I feel hurt. If my husband divorces me for another, I feel devastated.

If my high school steady makes a pass, I feel confused and offended. If my uncle attempts to sexually molest me, I feel terrified and violated.

The stronger the bond, the deeper the sense of betrayal, and consequently the greater the damage to trust.

Like Humpty Dumpty, the pieces of fractured trust will not fit back together the same way. There will be irreversible changes. However, healing can occur with new pieces growing to replace the broken ones. There is much that helping people can do to facilitate such healing. We can issue the invitation; we can create the climate; we can reinforce the response; and we can strengthen the resolve. What we can't do is take the risk.

The unavoidable paradox with fractured trust is that the healing can only begin as one takes the risk to trust again. While the damage can occur without one's cooperation, recovery cannot.

> *Humpty Dumpty climbed back up the wall,*
> *Recovering from wounds incurred by the fall,*
> *Accepting the challenge to turn life around,*
> *   after all...*
> *Who wants to live in pieces on the ground?*

Sticks and Stones

"Sticks and stones may break my bones but words can never harm me."

Maybe this old adage is a quick fix for hurt feelings on the playground, but in many of our life situations, it just doesn't hold true. I had someone call me a hypocrite recently. And it hurt.

Funny. I've been called other things that some would consider far worse: I've been called a fanatic, a fool, a Jesus freak, and a Holy Roller. Those never hurt. In fact I rather enjoy them as backhanded compliments.

A few times I've been called unprintable names that have attempted to link my ancestry to the canine family, have cast aspersions on my fidelity to my marriage vows, or even insinuated that I might be a hermaphrodite. While I wince at their coarseness, even these do not hurt.

But "hypocrite"? Hypocrite hurts.

I can't think of anything I want more than to be an effective witness for Jesus Christ. There is nothing for which I pray more earnestly, nothing for which I strive more diligently. So having the term *hypocrite* hurled in my face has a way of undermining my very existence. And like the predator senses the weakness of its prey, I think the person who called me a hypocrite knew that.

"Blessed are you," Jesus says, "when people insult you, persecute you and falsely say all kinds of evil against you because of me. Rejoice and be glad, because great is your reward in heaven, for in the same way they persecuted the prophets who were before you" (Matt. 5:11, NIV).

Hypocrisy is a very real and very ugly sin. But it is also an accusation that is often made falsely and therefore constitutes persecution. In such situations, I offer these observations:

1. When someone uses the word *hypocrite* it seems that what they really mean is "imperfect Christian." I don't

know about you, but while "hypocrite" hurts, I don't have any problem owning the description "imperfect Christian." Reframing it as such helps neutralize the sting.

2. I rarely hear the accusation, "hypocrite," used by a person who has a healthy relationship with Christ and a close connection with other believers. Because of this, I suspect that for the most part the one who throws out the word *hypocrite* like a trump card does so to avoid dealing with his or her personal standing before God.

   You see, if I have put a barrier between myself and God, the simplest way to keep that barrier in place is to negate anything that would force me to reevaluate my behavior in relation to God's standards. For example, the person who called me a hypocrite is a woman with a sad and unstable history concerning men, alcohol, and marriage.

3. We are often accused of being a hypocrite when we have taken an unpopular stand. I was called a hypocrite right after I had verbalized some boundaries that I needed to keep in place in my life. I did not at any point say that others had to adopt the same boundaries for themselves, but only that such boundaries were what I needed for my own mental health and well-being.

So, just why is it that we are blessed when people persecute us and falsely say all kinds of evil against us? Maybe it's because such persecution and false accusations have the effect of driving us to ruthless self-examination beneath the penetrating lens of the Holy Spirit.

And in light of that, I guess I only have to worry when being called a hypocrite doesn't hurt.

Wounds or Walls?

"Anytime Carpet Cleaners. May I help you?"

"Yes, I'd like to arrange to have my carpets cleaned, this Saturday if possible."

"Well, Mr. Smith doesn't work on Saturdays, but he could do it on Sunday."

The chill ran down my spine as my defenses shot up. Even though it was none of my business, I asked the question: "Why doesn't he work on Saturdays?"

"Well, he's a _____." My intuition was confirmed while the knot formed in my stomach. Mr. Smith, it seemed, was a member of a religious group that interprets the Old Testament laws regarding the Sabbath as literally binding for Christians. In a flood of adrenaline, I nearly hung up.

"What's the problem?" you might ask. "You want him to clean your carpets, not preach a sermon! You think he's going to teach them to roll up on Saturdays and refuse to work?"

And under uncluttered circumstances it wouldn't have been a big deal. But what Mr. Smith and his receptionist didn't know was that over the preceding months my personal life had been immensely complicated by another member of the same organization whose distorted practice of that belief system had left my spirit raw.

Consequently, simply hearing the name caused my knee to jerk.

Now, before you write me off as narrow-minded or judgmental, let me remind you that you have done likewise...

I've seen you do it, sisters, when you hear a man start to talk about biblical submission in marriage. Because you have been oppressed by its *mis*application, you turn off at its very mention.

I've seen you do it, brothers, when you meet me—a woman pastor. The veil drops over your eyes as you mentally back off, and the unspoken question hangs between us like a dense fog: *What kind of militant feminist agenda is she pushing?*

I hear it in the silence of certain colleagues when the word *evangelism* enters the dialogue. Inevitably somebody feels compelled to drag the stereotype out of the archives and say, "But it's not our style to knock on doors."

It's there, my fundamentalist friends, when the discussion turns to inclusiveness and you react to it as though it were synonymous with Unitarianism.

I could go on. But the point is, like my contact with the carpet cleaner, we all carry into current situations the memories of previous encounters that have some similarities to the present one. And because the previous situation has brought about pain, anger, or grief, we project those feelings onto the current one.

And our knee jerks.

Our wounds are very real, and we need to tend to those wounds and let them heal. It is also okay to be cautious. The old adage, "Fool me once, shame on you; fool me twice, shame on me," has some merit.

But, brothers and sisters, it is our eternal responsibility before God not to allow our wounds to develop into walls or our caution degenerate into accusation.

"Mrs. Mayer? Are you still there? Did you want to schedule your carpet cleaning for Sunday?"

I found my voice. "Actually, because of my own convictions, I'm not comfortable with Sunday. How about Monday?"

Horror Movies

Horror movies scare the daylights out of me.

Upon the few occasions I was foolish enough to watch one as a child, I'd invariably spend that night in my parents' bed. I was eighteen when my boyfriend took me to see *The Exorcist*, and afterwards I slept with a stuffed bunny for weeks. Even now, if I accidentally glimpse a horror scene during a preview I have an irrational urge to cross myself and recite the rosary...except I don't know the rosary.

So while I don't make a habit of watching them, it seems to me that the horror component of typical horror movies revolves around dead things that won't stay dead—zombies, vampires, mummies, ghosts—dangerous creatures who are supposed to have died, but who continue to haunt the living because they're not *really* dead.

Psychologically, the same scenario repeats itself in our lives. Often we are most terrorized and immobilized by some past occurrence that's supposed to be a dead issue, but instead keeps reaching out from its grave. It may be a guilty secret, an honest mistake, a destructive habit, an old grudge, or the silent shame borne by an assault victim. But what inevitably happens in many a person's life is that she or he mistakenly assumes such things are dead when they're only dormant...buried alive.

Among the most frequently voiced misconceptions concerning the therapeutic process is the idea that "all they do is dwell on the past and blame the parents for everything. Why dredge all that stuff up...aren't we supposed to forgive and forget and just get on with life?" Yeeesss...but...

Haven't you placed carefully wrapped leftovers in your refrigerator, forgotten about them, and then found them spoiled? In spite of the cool temperature, in spite of being sealed off from other perishables, eventually the stench of the spoiled food permeates the whole compartment, and if you don't act fast the good stuff is contaminated by the rotten.

And haven't you seen cuts and abrasions that on the surface seemed to be healing, but underneath were teeming with infection? Everyone knows that in such cases you can't cure the infection unless you reopen the wound.

Contrary to the old adage, ignoring something does not make it go away. Denial is not death. In order for a painful part of our past to die, it has to be killed. In order to kill it, we must do battle. And in order to do battle, we must confront it. Then and only then can we bury it and expect it to stay buried.

In his letter to the Corinthian church, the apostle Paul stresses how that which is sown does not come to life "unless it dies" (1 Cor. 15:36). If the seed does not die, it will not produce fruit. Newness can only happen after a death and a burial. On a spiritual level we symbolize this through baptism. However, we run into problems when we attempt to apply this principle in our day-to-day lives and personal histories because dying hurts and burial is hard work.

In order to bring that which is sown to life, we must do battle with the psychological zombies and emotional mummies so they can be killed and buried. Which in turn sets us free to newness: new options, new possibilities, and new depth in relationships without the icy fingers of not-yet-dead issues clawing at us from incontinent graves.

In horror movies the story reaches a resolution only after the protagonist successfully kills the frightening creature. In real life the death of old fears, memories, and resentments also brings a successful resolution. But left to themselves they usually don't die, only fester. Confronting them releases us from their grip, neutralizes their power, and allows us to forget "what lies behind and [strain] forward to what lies ahead" (Phil. 3:13).

ENJOYING PAIN

We live in an anesthetized society where the automatic response to pain, any pain, is to medicate it and be rid of it. But that conditioned reaction overlooks the fact that pain can be a very valuable indicator. What fascinates me about Hansen's Disease, commonly known as leprosy, is that the disfigurement results not from the leprosy bacillus itself, but from the secondary infections that set in and go unnoticed because of the body's insensitivity to pain.

Likewise, if we're too quick to numb ourselves emotionally we're liable to be vulnerable to more damage. All pain is not created equal and we'd all be a lot healthier if we'd make the time and take the risk to understand, rather than underestimate, our emotional pain.

There are times when pain is the result of a trauma. Bandages, stitches, casts, and slings all give witness to physical injuries that need to be protected from further damage while they heal.

Outside sources can also generate emotional pain, and though we can't always prevent such things from happening, we can usually learn to predict what kinds of situations might precipitate new pain. I know a lot of people who don't go to their high school class reunions. In fact, I'm one of them! That was not a happy time in my life, and I don't need fresh pain from old wounds. When emotional pain is from an outside source, there are times it makes sense to remove ourselves from that source.

Another way we experience pain is similar to the pain of sore, stiff muscles that have been forced to stretch beyond their previous limits. After I'd completed my one and only marathon (more years ago than I care to admit), I could hardly move for a week, and it felt great! My pain was my prize...my trophy reminding me of what I'd accomplished.

Then there's the pain that comes from withdrawal. If you haven't experienced it you've surely seen dramatizations of it. The addict who stops using a substance cold-turkey goes through nightmarish agony while the body reprograms itself to function without the drug. I've seen such pain over and over again in individuals who withdraw from a destructive relationship. A common pitfall with such pain is that the individual incorrectly concludes that the pain indicates he or she has made a mistake by terminating the relationship, when in fact it's far more similar to the pain experienced by a heroin addict trying to kick the habit.

Saving the best for last, I'd like to mention the pangs of childbirth. There is excruciating, yet exquisite, pain in giving birth. In this case, the pain is an intrinsic, inextricable part of the process...a process that brings forth something beautiful. So powerful is this process Jesus used it as a metaphor to prepare his disciples for their sorrow at his death, then joy of his resurrection: "When a woman is in labor, she has pain, because her hour has come. But when her child is born, she no longer remembers the anguish because of the joy of having brought a human being into the world. So you have pain now; but I will see you again, and your hearts will rejoice, and no one will take your joy from you" (John 16:21-22). There are junctures in our lives when we all, male and female, engage in some kind of spiritual birthing that is inevitably accompanied by pain.

Pain is communication, and learning to understand it as such can improve our spiritual and mental health. There are times when it means something is wrong, in which case it does need to be medicated, eliminated, or avoided. However, there are other times, such as with sore muscles, withdrawal from destructive relationships, and birthing processes, when pain indicates something is very, very right...in which case it needs to be endured, integrated, and even enjoyed.

HIDE 'N' SEEK

I hide things from my family.

I know. It sounds dishonest, or maybe even a little neurotic. But I assure you it's my only recourse. It all started because every time I needed a roll of tape...or a pair of scissors...or a memo pad...or a *sharpened* pencil with an eraser...or the church directory—there was none to be found.

See, these are all things I have conscientiously provided for communal convenience. They each have a parking spot near the area they will most likely be needed. But they keep disappearing.

For instance, somewhere in this household (probably in a toolbox out in the garage) there is a perfectly good pair of Chicago Cutlery scissors that should have never left the kitchen. I *really* miss them. Naturally no one in the house ever admits to having used any of the missing items. Apparently they just wander off of their own volition.

So I have duplicate items for my own personal use, which I hide. When one of the boys asks, "Mom, where is *the* tape?" I reply, "*The* tape is wherever the last person who used it set it down." When my husband calls up the stairs, "Honey, have you seen *the* scissors?" I simply say, "No."

It's not exactly a lie; I don't know where *the* tape is. I haven't seen *the* scissors. Now, I know where *my* tape is, and I've seen *my* scissors. They are safe in their hiding place, and I'm not about to let them be misused and lost.

David, extolling his fearless trust in the Lord, wrote: "For he will *hide* me in his shelter in the day of trouble; he will *conceal* me under the cover of this tent" (Ps. 27:5, emphasis mine). While seeking God's protection against his enemies, he prayed: "Guard me as the apple of the eye; *hide* me in the shadow of your wings" (Ps. 17:8, emphasis mine).

The words are pretty. But David didn't write them in pretty places. He was on the run from King Saul. His very life was in very real danger for a very long time. He most likely scribbled these words down on scraps of papyri while sitting on the hard, cold ground beside a waning campfire. Perhaps he paused periodically to wipe the tears from his eyes or shake his fist at heaven. Then he'd finish the words that would live long after he was gone and hide them in some worn-out satchel before moving on.

Our lives will never be trouble-free. We'll need something and it won't be there. We'll look for things and not be able to find them. We'll give, and it won't be received. We'll try, and it will seem not to matter. People will disappoint us; friends will betray us; enemies will pursue us.

But our soul is protected by our Lord, hidden in the shadow of his wings, concealed in his tabernacle. We are safe.

> *He hideth my soul in the cleft of the rock*
> *That shadows a dry thirsty land;*
> *He hideth my life in the depths of his love*
> *And covers me there with his hand,*
> *and covers me there with his hand.*
>
> —Fanny Crosby

ONIONS AND TEARS

When I was growing up, my mother never cooked with onions. In fact, she still doesn't cook with onions. You can't slide them by her either. She can detect even the most microscopic mincing!

Anyway, since I grew up in an onion-free home, I didn't realize till I was out on my own and doing my own cooking that onions really do make your eyes water! When I used to watch cartoons of Popeye and Shorty crying while peeling onions, I thought it was just an irrelevant detail. I was amazed the first time I peeled an onion and experienced involuntary tears.

Resentment in relationships is like an onion. It grows quietly underground, virtually unnoticed until it's pulled into the light. In order to get to its source it has to be peeled back a layer at a time. Which brings tears.

With the couples I've counseled over the years, the two primary contributors I've found to resentment are unresolved anger and unrealistic expectations.

Unresolved Anger: Anger, when experienced, needs to be acknowledged and addressed quickly. When it isn't, it festers and freezes into resentment. Scripture tells us to "be angry but do not sin; do not let the sun go own on your anger" (Eph. 4:26). That certainly suggests that the sin is not with the anger itself, but with the resentment that results from allowing the anger to set and seethe.

Unrealistic Expectations: This goes hand in hand with the anger mentioned above, because sometimes anger springs from expectations that are not realistic. All too often a person places the undoable burden upon a spouse to "make me happy." Then when it doesn't happen, there is resentment.

Let me tell you about one young couple in particular who were struggling with resentment. Married just out of high school with a baby on the way, He and She had overcome some significant obstacles in the ten years hence. He was successful. She was gorgeous. The children were bright and beautiful. As husband and wife, they were totally committed to each other and sincerely desired to honor God.

When I asked him what he appreciated about his wife, he proceeded to list all the things she did for him: "She has supper on the table when I get home; she makes my lunches; she irons my shirts; she waits up for me when I work late...."

Now, there's nothing wrong with appreciating things that often get taken for granted. But this young man was married to an *extremely* intelligent, talented, creative woman who had put her own dreams and goals on hold for some time. He, in turn, had defined her role as someone who existed to make his life easier.

Her response was tremendous hurt and anger. She had spent a number of years stockpiling resentment *all the while never talking to him about those feelings.*

So together we peeled back through the onion. He corrected his philosophy about "wifing" and expanded his capacity for "husbanding."

She, on the other hand, corrected her expectations, realizing that it was not fair to insist her husband be her sole source of self-esteem. And she learned to tell him when she was angry about something that was (or was not) happening in their relationship.

We started with the thin, slick, brittle skin of that onion (the part that's hard to get a grip on). We peeled back through the thick, tough outer layers. We worked the more pliable, inner layers. And finally, when we got to the core, it was smaller, sweeter, more tender, and quite manageable.

And, oh yes, there were tears.

They didn't get a quick fix. They learned a process. And they discovered that at the core—underneath the resentment—there was still a lot of love.

A View from Crutches

I gave him my most convincing "You've *got* to be crazy!" look and parroted his words: "You're going to break the bone in my foot, put me in a cast up to my knee, and make me walk on crutches for six weeks for the sake of a *toe* that's a little crooked?!"

So he ran through it again. He showed me the x-ray, explained how it had healed wrong from a previous surgery, told me horror stories of how neglect could lead to crippling arthritis, warned me if I put any weight on that foot I'd have the same problem, then called in his partner who glanced at the x-ray and said all the same things.

So I put my affairs in order and went under the knife.

I thought I was prepared. I sort of had this idea that my life would just be business as usual, except I'd be on crutches. No big deal, right?

Wrong!

I didn't know what a cast could do to one's balance. I didn't know the maddening frustration of not being able to carry even the smallest item. I didn't know the sheer terror of staring at a stretch of slippery sidewalk between the myself and the door.

Six weeks on crutches easily qualifies for my personal list of Top 10 Most Miserable Experiences. While I was (more or less) prepared for the fact that I would not be able to walk on my left foot, I was not prepared for all the secondary complications that would create.

After just one day on crutches I began hurting in places where I didn't even know I had places! My biceps, triceps, and just-let-me-die-ceps all groaned in protest from the unaccustomed work. As I struggled with those crutches, literally counting the days till I would be rid of them, I realized my situation was a living allegory for the broader spectrum of any recovery process.

Some things have to be broken in order to heal.

From the alcoholic who bottoms out, to the womanizer whose wife finally says "no more" and leaves, to the cut-throat executive who loses everything, to the sinner who prostrates himself before God crying, "Wretched man that I am!" (Rom. 7:24), some things have to be broken in order to heal.

For different reasons all of us have learned to cope in less than perfect ways. And because of that, we have crooked places. Sometimes those crooked places do not interfere with our day-to-day functioning. And other times they can become a center of dysfunction that requires a whole lifestyle to revolve around them.

Some things have to be broken in order to heal.

And what we discover in the recovery process, as I discovered on crutches, the secondary effects of healing can be just as difficult, if not more so, than the primary problem.

Like the workaholic dad who realizes he's neglected his family too long and rejoins them. That is a good thing. However, he's likely to discover a wife and kids who have developed a routine that works just fine without him thank-you-very-much and that is disrupted by his involvement. The process of reestablishing balance does not happen complication-free.

Or consider the woman who decides to pursue some personal goals that have long been on hold. Again, a good thing. But the side effect may be a husband who feels neglected that his shirts aren't always ironed and resentful that supper's not always on the table.

Growth, recovery, and healing, are all good things, and are always good things. But just as my crutches (absolutely necessary to protect my foot) brought pain to my arms and shoulders, so the process of recovery can stress and stretch relationships.

But you know what? After I made it through the initial adjustment period, my arms were strong enough to support me ache-free. Which holds true in other healing processes as well.

THE KEY

I still carry the faded blue key to my parents' house.

I had it made my senior year of high school when I worked at Sears. There was this incredibly cute guy who worked at the key counter, and the moment I laid eyes on him I realized the gaping void in my life for lack of my own personal house key!

Twenty-five years later, that key remains on my key chain and goes everywhere I go. It has endured countless key ring weedings. It has outlasted at least a dozen other keys of residence. It has remained fast through no less than ten different vehicle keys. It has seen several office keys come and go.

It's made it through more than one car wreck. It has survived heaven-only-knows-how-many lost purse adventures. And it even found its way back to me once after being stolen in an armed robbery.

It means something to me. The key to my parents' house has become an important symbol. For instance:

It reminds me that I'm loved.

It reminds me that I always have someplace to go and somewhere to turn.

It reminds me of strengths and virtues born at home that have become my keys for survival.

It also reminds me of hang-ups born at home that are areas yet to be unlocked.

For better or worse, these qualities are constants that combine into my keys for problems, barriers, challenges, and opportunities.

Tune in to the climate of the Christmas season and you will find that it is saturated with sentiments of home.

Carolers sing about going home for the holidays. Television is punctuated with stories of emotional reunions. And the classic Christmas movie, *It's a Wonderful Life*, tells about a man who didn't realize how much home meant to him until a befuddled angel revealed to him how tragic home would have been without him.

Years ago Marjorie Holmes wrote a masterpiece entitled "At Christmas the Heart Goes Home." In it she shares how one Depression Christmas she and her adult siblings all managed to finagle crowded, bumpy, unheated rides from various parts of the country so they could all be together for the holy day. There were no presents, no trimmings, and no extras. But they were home.

She then draws a parallel between our instinctive yearning for home at Christmas and the story of a young couple from Nazareth who were mysteriously propelled towards their own hometown, Bethlehem.

There is indeed no place like home for the holidays. Yet for many survivors of divorce who are living out the complications of broken and blended families, nostalgic pictures of Christmas homecomings can be little more than the wistful longing for the used-to-be.

I am reminded of this as I hang up the phone from yet another conversation attempting to juggle the geographical and relational logistics required to ensure that everyone gets a piece of the children for Christmas. I swallow the lump in my throat and acknowledge, once more, that "home" did not turn out the way I planned.

But I have the key.

It reminds me that no detour can destroy the home we carry in our hearts. It reminds me that no disappointment can steal our ability to create home wherever we find love. And it reminds me that, thanks to Bethlehem, we have an eternal home that no upheaval can shake and no disaster can break.

So to all those who feel like home is scattered in pieces— to all whose homes did not turn out the way you planned— remember to use the keys of faith, hope, and love to recreate all the blessings home brings.

WINGS OF GRACE

The night before my mother-in-law died, my father-in-law left the hospital at twilight. He was alone, which was odd, for he'd usually traveled to the hospital with someone else during Mom's illness. But a series of missed connections left him driving by himself that day.

Approaching his car, he noticed something blue near the front wheel. A lost toy? A piece of broken plastic? Somebody's misplaced glove or discarded sandwich wrapper? As he got closer, it moved. More precisely, it fluttered.

How in heaven's name did a tired little parakeet manage to survive the dangerous jungle of metropolitan traffic and find its way into the parking lot of a large hospital? Did God send it?

Picture, if you will, a seventy-six-year-old man (with a bad back) chasing after a frightened, hungry parakeet with a windshield scraper and brown paper bag, all the while coaxing in German: "I gonna catch you, little birdie…yes I gonna get you." Not even a younger, more agile man could have outmaneuvered a bird that didn't want to be caught.

Apparently this bird wanted to be caught, because the little guy hopped into the bag as though returning to his mother's nest. Dad took him home, bought a cage, gave him food and water, then set him by the window where he could sing to the morning light.

A few days later, after losing his bride of fifty-eight years, he said to us, "Mebee you thin' Ih'm crazy, but I thin' God sen' me dat biurd so I would'na be alone."

Did God send the bird? Well, it certainly wouldn't be the first time God sent a bird to help his people.

There was the dove, of course, in Genesis 8. Noah had released it from the ark, and it returned with an olive branch which told Noah that the flood waters had receded from the earth. In Exodus 16 God sent quail to the children of Israel so they would not starve during their long wilderness journey.

Then there were the ravens in 1 Kings 17. While Elijah was hiding out in the Kerith Ravine, God commanded them to bring him bread and meat. (Which required greater faith—to believe that God would provide food through the birds, or to actually eat something that had been in a raven's mouth?!)

Yes indeed. If we read the Bible, God seems to have a thing for birds.

Did God send the bird to my father-in-law?

"If God did sen' me dat biurd—is not a vera good trade, ya know, a biurd fer a voman!" He chuckles at his wit, but my heart aches at the loneliness beneath his words.

He's never known life without her. Together they grew up in the same Yugoslavian village. Together they survived WW II. Together they endured deportment after the war during one of Yugoslavia's ethnic cleansings. Together they immigrated to America where, already in their forties, they learned a new language and built a new life. And together they raised three sons in a culture radically at odds with their Old World values.

Did God send the bird to my father-in-law?

Of course God sent the bird to my father-in-law!

How do I know that? Because in Matthew 10:29 Jesus says: "Are not two sparrows sold for a penny? Yet not one of them will fall to the ground apart from your Father." Maybe it's a stretch, but I figure if God keeps track of sparrows, then God surely must keep track of parakeets.

Did God send him the bird as a trade for his wife?

No. Our God is a loving and generous God who is eager to bless his children, not some sadistic despot exacting a pound of flesh for his mercies.

What about reincarnation?

Puh-leeze! While God loves and cares for all creatures, God is not in the business of recycling souls.

I believe God sent the parakeet to my father-in-law for the same reason he sent the dove to Noah, the quail to the Israelites, and the ravens to Elijah: as a symbol of hope, a message of encouragement, a sign that there are better days to come. Because, you see, as Birdie welcomes each new morning with a song, he reminds Dad that while "weeping may linger for the night...joy comes with the morning." (Ps. 30:5).

IV | WHEN YOU TRIP ON THE TIE THAT BINDS...

Working toward healthy relationships

SPRING CLEANING

There's an ancient masochistic ritual that I understand still survives in many parts of the world. It involves torturous labor, obsessive standards, compulsive routines, and neurotic motivation. It is progressive, predictable, debilitating, and ultimately self-defeating. Annually, sometime between the celebrations of Passover and Pentecost, countless proselytes rise up to practice this grueling, time-consuming, energy-draining, blood-sucking sacrament.

They call it "spring cleaning."

Housework is frustrating, to say the least. Don't you agree? As soon as you're finished, you have to start all over again. Personally, I'd much rather put effort into things that stay done. For instance, when I write an article, it stays written. I don't pull it up on my computer a few days later and find dust all over it and the words in disarray. However, since the need for cleaning simply won't go away, every new moon I break down and do just enough to get by. And here's what I notice:

Once I sort through the accumulated paraphernalia and make decisions about what to keep and what to discard...once I put things in their proper place...once I get the big items out of the way—in short—once I clear out the clutter, the actual cleaning is almost easy.

There are just some things in life that need ongoing attention: dishes, laundry, gardens, lawns, cars...and people. It would be nice if we could nail a relationship in place and not give it a second thought for the next twenty years, but it doesn't work that way. There needs to be routine maintenance and periodic spring cleaning.

First of all, you sort through and decide what to keep and what to throw away. You want to keep the memories, the unfinished business, the hard-won lessons, and the love. But sooner or later you'll need to discard the petty grudges, unrealistic expectations, and unreasonable resentments.

Next, you put your priorities in their proper place. Keep in mind that where (and with whom) you use your time, distribute your energy, and spend your money—in other words, where you "lay up your treasures"—says an awful lot about where your heart is.

Now you're ready to get the big items out of the way. Perhaps there are disabling secrets, deadly feuds, or deep, festering wounds creating solid, seemingly insurmountable walls. Whatever their nature or source, identify them and work towards resolving them.

Finally, you're ready to scrub, to dust, and to polish. Note here that all these tasks generate friction. Like household cleaning, relationship maintenance is far easier and less taxing if it's done routinely, before there's a pileup. And with the clutter out of the way, it can actually be enjoyable.

I don't know if spring cleaning is part of your agenda this year or not. But if it is, while you're beating rugs, scrubbing baseboards, shampooing carpets, waxing floors, washing walls, and delving into the nether world behind bureaus and beneath beds, stop and consider whether or not you have a relationship or two that could use similar attention.

STORMY MARRIAGE

I've spent a lot of hours with couples in marriage counseling. I also went through a divorce after fourteen years of marriage to my first husband. Consequently, I know through both professional and personal experience the disillusionment that can lie in wait behind the promise of happily ever after.

I believe that marriage was ordained by God to protect the family, provide a channel for grace, and to present us with a living metaphor of the eternal devotion between Christ and his church.

And even for those who disagree with that particular theology of marriage, there's no denying that cultures worldwide have long recognized marriage as an institution.

But marriage is also a *relationship*...a living, fluctuating, vulnerable relationship. And like all living things, if it is not properly nourished, it will become weak, sick, and eventually die. I'm not suggesting that it *might* falter. I am stating that it *will* falter. The key to surviving such episodes is that partners be committed enough to the institution of marriage to weather the storms of the *relationship* of marriage.

Let me share with you a snapshot from the life and times of my former pet, Shadrach. Shadrach was seventy-five pounds of glorious golden retriever with the presence of Aslan, the loyalty of Lassie, and the heart of Old Yeller. Unfortunately the roll of distant thunder could reduce this magnificent beast to a trembling, whimpering, unpredictable bundle of nerves.

I awoke one morning several years ago to discover that during the previous night's storm Shadrach had jumped out the window...right through the screen! I found him cowering under the bushes, muddy, bedraggled, and woebegone looking as if his sorry state of affairs was somebody else's fault.

Since Shadrach couldn't talk, I can only speculate as to his logic, but it must have gone something like this: *I'm trapped...I feel frightened...desperate...I'm going crazy...if I can just get away from where I am...then my problem will be solved and I'll be safe and happy.* And so in a frantic, futile attempt to escape the panic *within* him, he barreled headlong out of the security and into the storm.

Am I saying that Christians should *never* divorce? No. I've seen too many facets of too many marriages and can think of too many extenuating circumstances to make such a rigid, simplistic statement.

However, I have also seen far, far too many marriages where spouses think and behave like Shadrach.

There's a crisis—a crisis of finances, a crisis of midlife, a crisis of grief, a crisis of career, a crisis of identity or esteem. And in the midst of the crisis they begin to reason: *If I could just get out of the situation I'm in, then my problem will be solved and I'll be safe and happy.*

Consequently they rush headlong out of the frying pan into the fire, only to realize later that their unhappiness exits *with* them and cannot be exorcised by the legal exercise of divorce.

Hasty divorces are as unwise and unstable as hasty marriages. To initiate divorce proceedings without first considering alternatives and clarifying expectations is akin to Shadrach jumping out of the window to escape the storm. Those who do so will only set themselves up for posttraumatic grief and regret as well as another failed marriage in the future.

I believe it *is* possible to live happily ever after. However, it is a state achieved through choices and convictions, not circumstances.

Volleyball and Boundaries

I hate volleyball.

And it has nothing to do with not being good at it. I'm a lousy bowler, but I always have fun bowling. When it comes to running I'm more tortoise than hare, but jogging has been a part of my life for many years now. I'm not a sore loser—I don't have to be good at something to have fun with it. It's just that with volleyball there's a crucial difference.

You see, I am invariably assigned to a team that has at least one member who really, *really* likes to win. And it doesn't take this person very long to figure out that I'm not very good. Before you know it, he's all over me like white on rice every time the ball comes near me. Now, ordinarily I have no difficulty establishing my boundaries. But in this particular context I regress: my assertiveness exits, my reason evaporates, and my arms and legs become lead. In no time my rescuer and I are cooperating in an ineffective, dysfunctional relationship characterized by dependency, resentment, and lopsided responsibility.

And you know what? Our team nearly always loses because one person cannot continually cover the territory of two, and one person cannot continually carry the weight of two. Sooner or later the rescuer slips up, or wears out, or breaks down. Then we have not only lost the game, but we're angry, resentful, and blaming as well.

The same kind of scenario has been repeatedly observed in families of addiction. It's called "enabling." In a family system, the role of enabler is the one who helps, i.e., enables, a sick person to stay sick. An enabler neutralizes all motivation for a person with a problem to change by constantly rescuing the one with a problem from the natural, albeit unpleasant, consequences of his or her behavior.

In a chemically dependent family an example of an enabler would be a spouse who repeatedly calls in sick for a mate who is experiencing physical illness as a result of excessive drinking. Or a parent who intervenes on behalf of an offspring who is suffering the logical consequences of substance abuse—for example, bailing him out of jail, or loaning her money time and again when she mismanages her finances. In such situations the relationships become progressively dysfunctional and mutually dependent.

Although these roles are more glaring and rigid in chemically dependent, biological families, similar dynamics have been observed in many organizations, including the workplace and church congregations. Dysfunction comes in many shapes and sizes, and unfortunately has many aliases. Especially in the church context where we diligently strive to "give a cup of cold water" and "turn the other cheek," it's all too easy for enabling to masquerade as virtues...virtues like:

Support: True support will uphold constructive behaviors while allowing destructive behaviors to collapse. In contrast, enabling cultivates the sickness at the expense of the health.

Help: The difference here is that genuine help encourages one to outgrow the helper. Help that is enabling fosters dependence.

Forgiveness: In order for forgiveness to be forgiveness it must never diminish the damage. Theologically, we make a mockery of Christ's sacrifice and atonement if we do not acknowledge the magnitude of our transgression. Enabling has no common ground with forgiveness, for enabling pretends no harm has been done and refuses to admit, let alone address, the problem, overlook it, let it slide, or shrug it off.

Confused as to whether or not you're enabling? Here are some checkpoints: If your person-with-a-problem is aware of it, working on it, and showing measurable improvement, it's unlikely you're enabling.

Are you talking about it? If ever you find yourself covering up and keeping secrets, consider it a sign of enabling.

Finally, if your actions help your person-with-a-problem accept responsibility for his or her behavior, then it's not enabling because an enabler's so-called "help" provides infinite excuses to blame others.

My volleyball illustration is not a perfect parallel. In a game like that the problem is obvious and more easily corrected, whereas in relationships enabling is more subtle, enmeshed, and debilitating. But one similarity does hold true: As long as enabling continues, everyone loses.

YOUR TEENAGER'S DIRTY LITTLE SECRET

As I glanced out from the pulpit one Sunday morning, I caught a teenager in the act. Flustered and embarrassed by the discovery, he tried to hide it. But I know what I saw. And although he'd probably deny it if confronted, I'm an eyewitness to the fact: He was *listening* to me.

Is it possible that I am such a scintillating, captivating speaker that he was mesmerized by my wit, wisdom, and insight? I suppose it's possible…but unlikely. No, I think this young man's attentiveness had more to do with the simple and encouraging truth that our teenagers absorb a whole lot more than we often give them credit for. They listen to us on the sly…they follow our instructions when we're not looking…behind closed doors they repeat our advice to troubled friends.

All too often parents of teenagers assume (or fear) that their kids afford them no credibility whatsoever. So the logical parental response to that assumption is to increase the amount of instruction and restriction in an effort to extend protection to vulnerable young lives. And while there's certainly enough out there to tempt and confuse kids, such tightened control carries two very costly risks.

First of all, the more independent, spirited teen will respond by accelerating his attempts to establish an individual identity separate from that of his parents. In other words, he'll rebel.

The more insecure, passive teen will very likely comply, but in future situations where such control is absent (say, for instance, a college campus) he or she is far more likely to either crack under the pressure, or go into a tailspin, overdosing on experimentation.

I'm of the opinion that a certain amount of rebellion among teenagers is not only inevitable, but healthy. During the years of shifting from dependence to independence there's bound to be some grinding of the gears. But that's okay; it'll get smoother.

You see, the point is, when we overprotect our kids, we fail to prepare them. This task of establishing identity is one that must be accomplished. If it doesn't happen during adolescence, it's liable to happen at midlife. And I'm much rather see a fifteen-year-old acting like a rebellious adolescent than a fifty-year-old acting like a rebellious adolescent!

In speaking of rebellion here, I'm not endorsing destructive choices such as drug and alcohol use, criminal activity, premarital sex, or occult involvement. Neither am I suggesting that parents allow their own values and convictions to be disrespected. For example, as long as our boys live under our roof, there are certain standards they must accept including the movies they watch, the video games they play, the music they listen to, and the pictures they post on their bedroom walls. And, oh yes, Sunday morning church attendance is mandatory.

Acceptable rebellion would include things as curfew negotiation, pierced ears, unconventional haircuts, trendy (though not indecent) clothing, as well as differing views on society, politics, and religion.

Some time after the incident mentioned at the opening of this essay occurred, I attended the same young man's graduation open house. Keep in mind, this was a cocky kid. But in looking through his senior memory book I noticed that listed under the heading "People Most Admired" were the words, "My Parents."

So don't panic. As long as nothing is too sacred to be questioned or discussed... as long as you practice what you preach...as long as you help keep your kids connected with other caring adults, the odds of your teen successfully resolving the transition from adolescence to adult are in your favor.

And watch your teenagers the next time they think you're not looking. They're probably doing something responsible behind your back.

WHEN THE EMPEROR WEARS NEW CLOTHES TO CHURCH

Remember the story, "The Emperor's New Clothes"?

There was once an emperor so vain that two con artists were able to trick him into believing they were magic tailors who could weave a suit so exquisite and magnificent that only the wise and worthy could see it. It would be invisible to the simple-minded.

When the emperor inspected the "finished" suit, he of course saw nothing. But rather than have his subjects believe he was simple-minded, he raved over the beautiful, rich cloth and lustrous jewels.

Next, he arranged for a grand procession in which to parade his new clothes. The crowds, fearful they would be exposed as simple-minded, oohed and aahed over the invisible suit, except for one little boy, who cried out, "But the emperor has no clothes on!"

This fairy tale by Hans Christian Anderson stands as a parable for the church today. Join a congregation, any congregation. Denomination is of no consequence. Before long, you will start receiving clues as to who runs the church. It may be a senior person, junior person, male person, female person, lay person, or staff person.

But tragically, too often, this emperor person is is blind to his or her own character flaws and tends to exercise influence and power according to a personal agenda.

And nobody tells him he's "naked."

The other parishioners, fearful of repercussions, fearful of appearing judgmental, fearful of somehow looking simple-minded, take a passive stance and say, "Oh, that's just the way she is."

But no one tells her she's "naked."

Issues become inflated, decisions become power

struggles, molehills become mountains, and newcomers become history.

Yet, no one cries out that someone is "naked."

Let's go back to the fictional emperor: The man was parading naked in front of the whole town! That is not, by any stretch of the imagination, healthy behavior. Did those in the crowd who refused to name the truth do him any favors? Did they really have the emperor's best interests at heart?

According to the fable, they were primarily concerned with how they would be perceived. The only act of genuine caring came from the young boy who innocently cried out the truth: "But the emperor has no clothes on!"

When we passively allow dysfunctional, unhealthy behavior in our midst without naming the problem, we are not acting out of love at all, but rather out of a codependent need to maintain our own comfort level.

Am I advocating finger pointing and scapegoating? Not at all. I'm advocating redemption. Hear the words of the Amen, the faithful and true Witness: "For you say, 'I am rich, I have prospered, and I need nothing.' *You do not realize that you are wretched, pitiable, poor, blind, and naked....* I reprove and discipline those whom I love. Be earnest, therefore, and repent" (Rev. 3:17-19, emphasis mine).

When certain people dominate congregations, creating fear, strife, and division, we need to tell them they're "naked."

Interesting enough, in Hans Christian Anderson's story, the emperor realized that the boy spoke the truth, but was so ashamed he'd been fooled that he pretended all the people were wrong and kept on marching down the street.

Sometimes that happens. One can be told he's naked and he'll refuse to acknowledge the truth.

But sometimes she "anoints her eyes" and has "ears to hear." The Spirit gets through; a hardened heart is broken;

conviction leads to repentance; freely given grace is received; redemption comes full circle.

And isn't that what the gospel is all about?

HOW TO SILENCE A NAGGING WIFE

It was 9:37 Saturday night, and I was tired. As I made my way towards the bed, which already contained one husband (who was either asleep, or pretending to be), I stumbled on the pillows carelessly shoved into my path, eyed his recently discarded clothes piled on my side of the bed, noticed a pair of size 12s where they shouldn't be...and decided there would be no mercy:

"*Horst!* Can't you even take a few seconds to just put things away before you get in bed? I'm tired too. What makes you think I want to pick up after you before I get into bed at night? You don't need to dump the pillows on the floor right where I get in; you could at least move them out of the way so I don't have an obstacle course between me and the bathroom...

"Besides that, you kicked off your shoes right in the middle of the room where one of us is bound to trip over them. And what's with these clothes? We have a huge walk-in closet with plenty of space for dirty laundry. Why can't you put your things where they belong without leaving it for me to do?! You just shoved everything aside and crashed as if you're the only one who's had a hard day. At least you don't have to preach in the morning. I can't even get in bed without moving your stuff!"

To emphasize this point, I tossed his jeans on top of his head and crawled into bed where I continued my tirade: "I think it was really selfish and inconsiderate of you to leave a mess for me to deal with." With that, I flounced over in a huff and listened to several seconds of silence, which only agitated my already bad temper.

"Horst, are you awake?"

"Uh-huh."

"Well...aren't you going to *say* anything?"

"Goodnight, Beautiful. I love you."

What's a contentious woman to do?

I rolled over and spooned up behind him, wrapped my arms around his big, warm body and said: "Goodnight, honey. I love you too."

"A soft answer turns away wrath, but a harsh word stirs up anger" (Prov. 15:1).

A STEPFAMILY SHOPPING

I'd noticed them earlier wheeling their cart through the store: angry father, anxious mother, agitated boys. But honestly, I wasn't lurking in the shadows trying to eavesdrop. I was just waiting on the clerk to get my wallpaper. Still, I heard it all:

"Jason! I told you to keep your hands off!" (Funny how you can *hear* clenched teeth.)

"You didn't say anything to Brian when he picked it up, Bob!"

TWHACK!! "You're done, boy, do you hear me? Done!"

"I know, I know, no TV, no allowance, no friends, no nothing...I'm done."

Stepfamily. It was written all over them. And yes, I know that "blended family" is the preferred term. But tell me, does the above scenario sound very "blended" to you?

I received a call recently from the director of a home for unwed mothers. A former client of mine was seeking services and had signed a release. Did I remember Candy? I remembered her well. I remembered laboring long and hard with her parents on their marriage. I remembered the father, an alcoholic who blossomed from denial...to faith in Christ...to sobriety.

I also remembered the insecurity and confusion of Candy, then ten. Offspring of her mother's first marriage, she was adopted by this man at age three—just after her younger sister was born.

I remembered Dad admitting he just didn't *feel* for Candy what he *felt* for his natural daughter. I remembered telling him, "Candy needs your physical affection and verbal affirmation. And if you don't give it to her, she'll eventually find males who will."

That was nine years ago. This is Candy's second pregnancy. She has no idea who the father is.

Stepparents who live with their children-by-marriage are in an incredibly complex, difficult situation: The kids in the home experience a fresh wave of grief over the loss of their parents' marriage with each developmental milestone.

Stepdads whose own children live with the ex-wife often have such deep grief over that loss that attempts to bond with their wife's kids creates a sense of betrayal towards their own.

And stepmoms usually have a disproportionate burden of child-rearing responsibilities with stepkids who are frustrated because it's Dad they want to be with, not his new wife.

No wonder God hates divorce (see Mal. 2:16).

There's all kinds of good information available on how to blend stepfamilies, and I recommend you read it. I have nothing new to offer in the way of solutions. What I want to do is underscore the urgency.

Stepparents, time is not on your side. There is no time to take it easy, get your head together, or hang loose before you act. Young lives are hanging in the balance. What you do (or don't do) in the next few years will dramatically impact the trajectory of those lives. You don't have time to wait for the want-to to catch up to the need-to. This is one area where it is imperative that you make some decisions about doing right, then trust God to pull your emotions into harmony with those decisions.

Meanwhile, back at the store...I forgot about my wallpaper, walked up to Bob, gave him my business card and said: "It sounds like there's a lot of pain here. I can help if you'll let me. Give me a call."

I'm ashamed to confess, that is not what I did.

But I will next time.

WHEN A GOOD THING GOES BAD

Springtime.

Dogwoods and lilacs are in bloom; robins feather their nests; bunnies beget more bunnies; and a young man's fancy turns to love.

During springtime, church calendars fill up with the wedding dates of young couples eager to pledge their troth to one another. As I hang up the phone and reach for my appointment book to schedule a premarital counseling session for yet another starry-eyed bride and groom, I think to myself: *They have no idea.*

Don't get me wrong. In terms of my favorite pastoral functions, weddings rank right up there with baptisms and baby dedications. It's just that I know all too well that out of all the "I do's" that are spoken, many a bride or groom will eventually say, "I did then, but I don't now." And there's nothing sadder than when a good thing goes bad.

There is an often-overlooked Bible story about a starry-eyed young couple. David and Michal were society's darlings. He was a handsome war hero and future king of Israel. She was a princess, King Saul's second daughter. Even though their marriage was arranged according to the custom of the day, Scripture records twice in 1 Samuel 18 that Michal loved David. And since David had to slay a hundred men to win her, it is reasonable to conclude he *wanted* to marry her.

After the nuptials, we find in 1 Samuel 19 that King Saul is still determined to kill David, even though David is now his son-in-law. So David's adoring wife, Michal, helps her husband escape, and even plants the life-sized family idol in their bed as a decoy. When confronted by her father, she lies and tells him that David threatened to kill her if she did not help him.

For at least the next ten years, David plays a deadly game of cat and mouse with his deranged father-in-law. During that time, some significant things happen—and don't happen—that contribute to this good thing going bad.

King Saul gives Michal to another man to be his wife—Paltiel, son of Laish of Gallim. And David takes six additional wives. We have no idea if there was any contact, or attempted contact, between David and Michal during this time.

When David officially ascends the throne, one of his first demands is that his long-lost wife be returned to him: "Give me back Michal, for I bought her with the lives of one hundred Philistines" (2 Sam. 3:14, LB).

How did Michal feel about it? Scripture doesn't tell us directly, but it does give us some clues. We know, according to 2 Samuel 3:16, that her husband, Paltiel, grieved deeply over losing her. Then in 2 Samuel 6:16, we are told that as Michal watched from a window while the ark of God returned to Jerusalem with David leaping and dancing before the Lord she "despised [David] in her heart." Later she compares him to one of the foolish ones who shamelessly uncovers himself.

In 2 Samuel 6:20-22, David retaliates with cutting words, reminding her that he's the king and he will do just as he pleases, and if she doesn't like it, there are plenty of women who do. The last we hear of Michal is that she had no children to her dying day (v. 23).

There is just nothing sadder than a good thing gone bad. Here we have these idealistic young lovers who were considered a perfect match, but a few years later they are hurting each other with spiteful, hateful, words.

Where did they go wrong? In exactly the same areas young couples go wrong today:

1. *They entered their marriage with unrealistic expectations.* Michal wanted a hero. David was handsome and

popular, the catch of the county. Snagging David would make Michal the belle of the ball and the envy of all her peers. David wanted a princess. Marrying Michal would give him an in with the royal family, seal his position, and perhaps smooth over the turbulence with the man he would replace as king. David and Michal did to some degree what many young men and women do today when seeking a marriage partner. They came up with their personal blueprint of "Ideal Mate" and superimposed it on each other.

2. *They entered their marriage with unfinished family business.* Granted, where David and Michal are concerned, this is largely conjecture on my part. But think about it: Michal was her father's second choice; King Saul had originally offered the older sister, Merab, to David in marriage. Had Michal grown up in her sister's shadow? Was marrying David, to some degree, an attempt to win her father's approval?

And remember, David was the youngest of eight boys. None of his older brothers was exactly happy that the runt of the litter had been chosen to be Israel's king. In fact, when David offered to go fight Goliath, his eldest brother, Eliab, called him presumptuous and evil (1 Sam. 17:28). I have to believe that David's formative years were filled with attempts to prove himself. Was Michal just one more prize to win?

David and Michal, like many couples today, entered their marriage with unfinished family business, each wanting the other to fix his self-esteem and fill the void left by unmet needs from their families.

3. *They allowed circumstances to come between them.* David and Michal were swept up in circumstances beyond their control. David didn't choose the life of a

fugitive. Michal didn't choose to be given to another man in marriage. Neither had control over those turns of events. They were like many couples today who do not have control over circumstances: The real issue is not what happens *to* us, but rather how we *respond* to what happens to us.

Perhaps Michal grieved over lost love and lost youth. But instead of accepting her pain with grace and courage, she turned on David with venomous spite in 2 Samuel 6:20: "How glorious the king of Israel looked today: He exposed himself to the girls along the street like a common pervert!" (TLB).

And what about David? Does he honor the wife of his youth? Does he speak words of understanding and conciliation? Not at all. In 2 Samuel 6:21, he rubs it in that he has displaced Michal's family's dynasty and gloats that other women are attracted to him. Afterwards, he totally rejects Michael.

How do I know that? Because 2 Samuel 6:23 says Michal remained childless. Some biblical commentators will point to that and claim that God was extinguishing Saul's line. But I think the reason for Michal's barrenness is much simpler. I think David and Michal lived out their days under the same roof, husband and wife in name only.

Marriage is a good thing. But unrealistic expectations, unfinished family business, and reactions to unhappy circumstances can all combine to make many a good thing go bad. Identifying and addressing these issues, refusing to allow circumstances to come between you, and allowing God to take over your marriage can not only prevent a good thing from going bad, but also rescue one that has.

WHEN SILENCE ISN'T GOLDEN

My dog has a funny way of communicating. Whenever he needs something, he comes to me, parks his little caboose at my feet, and then just looks at me with great expectations. So I start guessing...

"What is it, Yogi? Food?" Silence.

"Do you want to go to bed?" Silence.

Hmmm...maybe he's been watching Lassie *again:* "Is it Timmy? Is Timmy in danger?" Silence.

"How about outside? Do you need to go outside?" Yip, yap, skip, scamper to the door. Depending on what he wants at the moment, the point at which he responds will change. The process, however, never changes. Invariably Yogi waits for me to guess what he needs.

Any communication process involves a sender and a receiver. And unfortunately many senders do not give clear messages to their receivers. They leave them guessing what they need. Here are some ways it happens:

Silence. I know people (and so do you) who use silence as an ineffective way to communicate hurt or anger. Have you heard this before?

"What's wrong?"

"Nothing."

"Why are you so quiet?"

"I just don't have anything to say (sniff)."

"Then why are you crying?"

"It's nothing."

"I know you're upset, so tell me what's wrong!"

"Nothing."

There is a time when silence is golden. There are also times when silence is a counterproductive method of communication that leaves the receiver guessing (not to mention frustrated).

Sarcasm. This one hits a little too close to home. When it comes to ineffective communication, sarcasm has always been my personal dysfunction of choice!

But the problem with sarcasm is that it gives a dual message. By definition, sarcasm is "a mocking remark utilizing statements opposite to the underlying meaning."

For example: A kid accidentally knocks a can of paint over while working on a project, and the supervisor says: "Oh, you're a big help!" A student receives a poor grade on an assignment and is told, "I can see you're going to be a great scholar!"

In sarcasm the words used do not match the message delivered, which leaves the burden upon the hearer to figure out what is really being said.

Secrecy. While this is a little bit like silence, it's more specific. With secrecy the sender intentionally withholds information about a particular issue. An area where this can be especially confusing is in a marriage where one partner is suffering the posttraumatic effects of sexual abuse.

A survivor of sexual abuse often has repressed memories of that abuse. Marriage, with its accompanying permission and expectations concerning sexual intimacy, can trigger those memories and dredge up old pain. Survivors who feel a lot of fear and shame may not be comfortable divulging their history to their spouse. However, that leads to another problem, because in such cases he or she often withdraws without explanation, and the spouse is left guessing: "Is she mad?" "Is he having an affair?" "Did I do something wrong?" "Doesn't she love me anymore?" "Doesn't he find me attractive?"

Silence, sarcasm, and secrecy—all are ways of sending messages that are at a high risk for misinterpretation because they leave it up to the hearer to guess what is really being communicated.

I suppose I shouldn't be too hard on Yogi for expecting me to guess what he needs. He is, after all, a dumb animal. However, since we humans are made in the very image of God who *spoke* creation into existence, it is our privilege—and responsibility—to communicate clearly.

STOP! IN THE NAME OF LOVE

Generally speaking, I'm a cautious driver.

I come to a full and complete stop at stop signs even if I'm out in the boondocks and there's not another car in sight. I don't pass on yellow lines. I always buckle up—even when I'm in the back seat and it's not required by law. I never drive (more than 20 miles) over the speed limit. And up until I moved to the City of Stoplights, I didn't run red lights.

It's true. In the six years I've lived in Kokomo I have probably slid through more intersections on orange lights than I had in the previous twenty-four years of my driving history.

I live exactly two miles from the church. Two miles. It should be a five-minute drive. However, with six stoplights between me and thee, it's ten minutes, minimum.

Kokomo High School is exactly three miles from our house. Three miles and nine stoplights. Once (and only once) I hit no red lights en route. It took eight minutes. With stops, add another ten. Multiply that eighteen-minute drive by three round trips a day (not uncommon with two teenagers) and that adds nearly two hours of driving to my already overloaded schedule.

I used to slow down when the light turned yellow. Now I speed up.

This is not a lesson on driving. It's a lesson on empathy.

"Remind the people...to slander no one, to be peaceable and considerate, and to show true humility toward all men"(Titus 3:1-3, NIV). Scripture makes it clear that God's community of faith is to be a community of understanding. So before we condemn other's behavior—other's lifestyle, other's sin—we need to stop, in the name of love, and consider the particular mix of circumstances, hardships, and frustrations he or she is going through.

It's easy for the person who's never gone hungry to condemn the thief who steals for food. It's easy for the able-bodied person who's always been able to work to criticize the disabled for needing public assistance. It's easy for the bright, well-educated to person to vilify the disadvantaged for poor choices about habits, budgets, and priorities. It's easy for those of us who have known much love to shake our heads at those who are fooled by its substitutes.

The fact that Kokomo has a surplus of stoplights doesn't make it right to run them. But living with the frustration of that surplus of stoplights does make me a little less self-righteous about the driving faults of others. In fact, it reminds me of the anonymous, ambiguous, long-lost proverb of questionable origin: "Each one travels to the beat of a different drum down a long and winding road with many stoplights. Before you cast stones at those who take the road less traveled, drive a mile in Kokomo."

LATE CHRISTMAS CARDS

If you ever want to find out who your true friends are, just send out your Christmas cards late.

Usually I'm one of those moderately compulsive people who has her shopping done by Halloween and her cards in the mail the day after Thanksgiving.

This year was different, however. Due to a series of unexpected events, Christmas was only a week away before I was frantically licking envelopes. With a little luck, my cards reached their respective destinations by New Year's.

What I noticed though, is that I didn't receive as many cards as in Christmases past. "Aha!" said I. "All these years I thought my old friends stayed in touch out of *loyalty*, when all along it was apparently just *reciprocity*."

Social scientists have advanced what's called the "Social Exchange Theory," which assumes individuals engage in a system of mental bookkeeping, continually appraising a relationship in terms of the flow of rewards and relative costs. So in view of our illustration, the Social Exchange Theory might translate into behavior as follows:

"Let's see…we'd better get a card out to the Millers; they sent us one. Don't forget the Bowmans; they always have something for us. And Mrs. Hoffer gave us those cookies, so we need to take her something."

Sound familiar? My college friends and distant cousins aren't the only ones who allow reciprocity to regulate their Christmas lists and relationships. You and I do too, at least to some degree. So the most effective way I know to constructively apply the principle of reciprocity is to be on the initiating end of it, i.e., to be *pro*active, rather than *re*active.

When we do this, first of all we claim our choices free from the pressure of others' expectations. On a personal level, this promotes independence, builds self-confidence, and enhances decision-making skills—all important qualities for effective leadership.

Secondly, we position ourselves to impact others in a positive, motivating way. For example, in group dynamics the most valuable interaction is born out of reciprocity. As one person opens up, others are encouraged to do likewise. Trust develops, understanding expands, intimacy evolves, and growth results.

You can see how placing yourself on the initiating end of reciprocity in relationships has both individual and corporate advantages. And this is nothing new, by the way. A long time ago, Jesus, while speaking to a large crowd from a hillside, advised that whatever we wanted others to do for us, we should do for them (Matt. 7:12).

Traditionally, the church has distilled this teaching down to a rule (you know, the "golden" one) and has tended to teach it in a rather flat, linear, dogmatic fashion. And while this principle certainly works as a moral standard for behavior, I think that application limits its impact and dilutes its power.

You see, I suspect that Jesus understood reciprocity. And I further suspect he knew that "doing unto others" would have the very rich potential of setting off a chain reaction of love, joy, peace, patience, kindness, goodness, faithfulness, and self-control—all the building blocks for peace on Earth and good will towards men.

Which brings me back to Christmas cards.

If reciprocity indeed holds true, I suspect my long-distance friends, after receiving my delinquent greetings, will reinstate my name on their Christmas card list.

Which means I'll have to be sure and send them a card the following year.

Talking to a Wall

Recently I paid a visit to someone in the county jail. Upon inquiring at the reception desk, I was directed towards an intercom on a wall at the far side of the room. The posted instructions read: "Push button and speak directly into speaker." So, pushing on the button, I gave my name, church, name of inmate, reason for visit... asked a few questions, made some clarifying comments, preached a sermon (not really), released the button, and waited.

...and waited...and waited....and waited.

After a couple of l-o-n-g minutes, a man walked up to the speaker, pushed the button, let go, waited for a beep, *then* stated his name, organization, etc.

I turned to two young men who'd witnessed the whole thing and stated the obvious: "So after you push the button, you're supposed to let go and wait for a response?" They grinned and nodded.

I had to admit it was pretty funny. "And you guys just sat there and let me...talk to a wall?"

"I feel like I'm talking to a wall!" It's one of my favorite colloquialisms. My guess is you've used it too...

Wives have used it after trying to relay the day's events to a husband with a remote control in his hand. Parents have used it after giving instructions to a kid with a Walkman plugged into his ears. Teachers have used it after extolling the value of reading, only to have students ask, "Have they made that into a cartoon yet?"

And pastors (though they seldom say it aloud) may wonder on Sunday afternoon: *Am I talking to a wall?*

"I feel like I'm talking to a wall." Isn't it funny how we say that as though the wall is entirely to blame? What can we learn from my conversation with the wall?

First of all, if we want to invite dialogue, we need to issue the invitation, and then wait for confirmation that the invitation has been accepted. The guy who followed me at the jail did just that. Unlike me, he made sure his call had been received before he delved into his agenda.

Secondly, if the initial query brings no feedback, make no assumptions. There are a host of reasons why a listener might not receive a signal. In one of her prayer-poems Ruth Harms Calkin describes her irritation, frustration, and suspicions when an acquaintance did not return her greeting at a bus stop. Ruth had mentally tried and convicted the other woman of snobbery, when she turned and, with tears in her eyes, said, "Please forgive me! I didn't see you. We've just learned our little boy has leukemia." If you feel like you're talking to a wall, it could be that "wall" is going through some tough times.

Thirdly, we need to evaluate the manner in which we sent the message. Did we make a mistake in the process? In word choice? In mechanics? When I sent my message into the intercom the second time, I made changes in the mechanics and timing.

Fourthly, don't look for someone else to blame. I really was joking when I insinuated the observers of my conversation with the wall were responsible for my silliness. But all too often when we feel we're not being heard, we look for a scapegoat.

And finally, we need to always remember that just because we're talking, doesn't mean we're communicating.

V | WHEN YOU COME TO A CROSSROADS...

Making changes and accepting limitations

TAKING THE LONG WAY HOME

Junior high years during the late '60s were hard on kids, I think. Especially girls. The still-intact school dress codes made recess activities downright immodest. While most of us were too old for "Lassie League," state-mandated school athletic programs for girls were still a few years off in the future. We were expected to sit with our knees together, but weren't allowed to wear nylons. We were beginning to have complexion problems, but were too young for make-up. We'd started our periods, but couldn't yet fill out our bras. None of us had actually retired our dolls, but we'd've died before admitting we still played with them. During the day we'd primp in front of the mirror, gossip on the telephone, and bat our eyes at the boys. Then at night we'd don our footed PJs and crawl into bed hugging our teddy bears.

It was during my seventh grade year that I used to walk to junior choir practice on Thursday afternoons with my friends, Debbie and Susie. We only lived about a mile from the church, so it wasn't a terribly long walk. However, we always managed to make it longer because between our houses and the church was a creek. And it was much more fun to follow the creek than the sidewalk!

Something about that creek gave us three in-betweeners permission to abandon pretense and ignore expectations in a swan song of childhood. Oblivious to the clock and unconcerned with the consequences, we'd hoist up our skirts and take the long way to church and home again.

For a short stretch of time we'd follow that stretch of creek and stretch our imaginations, pretending to be Maid Marian on a reconnaissance mission, Sacagawea leading Lewis and Clark to safety, or Annie Oakley tracking hostile Indians. We did this in the dead of winter, which means parts of the creek were frozen...and parts weren't. Making our way along the stepping stones that jutted out, we explored every crevice, inspected every critter, and collected a king's ransom in pink quartz and fool's gold. Predictably, we'd lose balance plunging a booted foot into the icy water which occasionally crept up over a bare knee.

Eventually we'd arrive at choir practice—usually late, often wet, always careful to avoid Mrs. Pauzek's disapproving eyes. We'd inconspicuously slide into our seats (well, as inconspicuously as three giggly twelve-year-old girls can be), and for about forty-five minutes concentrate on learning the songs.

Adolescence isn't the only life stage where we feel we're straddling two worlds. People going through divorces experience a twilight zone of status—not quite married, yet not quite single. Many workers enter retirement while still too young to collect benefits or qualify for senior discounts. Then there is the grueling transition involving a terminal illness. Each day dawns with the indisputable reality that death is hovering just around the corner as well as the uncompromising uncertainty of when it will call in its grim marker.

While in the midst of such in-between times we often wish we could fast-forward through them. Yet, like the proverbial butterfly must struggle to be released from her cocoon, it's neither possible nor wise to circumvent the process. So instead of looking for shortcuts, take the long way home. Explore the path, stretch your limits, take some risks, break some rules, and give yourself permission for "regression in service of the ego" as my psychology professor used to say.

Even though my friends and I weren't model choir members, to our credit we never skipped out entirely and we always returned the following week. Perhaps the biggest miracle of all—we actually learned to sing.

Near the end of my seventh grade year my family moved to a new house a few miles farther from the church, which eliminated the creek option. By high school we girls had traded in our knee socks for panty hose, our comic books for *Sixteen Magazine*, and our wading boots for stacked heels. Debbie and Susie even developed cleavage. In short— despite all our fears, anxiety, and impatience—we grew up.

Life is full of crossroads requiring us to make transitions and accept limitations. Taking the long way home can alleviate anxiety and give us time to adjust.

IN THE MIDDLE OF A MESS

It's not that I haven't moved before. I've moved lots of times. But nine years in one place was the longest I'd lived anywhere in my adult life, and I managed to acquire more...stuff than I had the last time I moved.

I also have had a child in those nine years who has managed to build up his own collection of...stuff. And since my husband had lived alone for some time, he too had accumulated a significant amount of...stuff.

So here I am, in the middle of a mess.

Have you ever embarked upon a major project with high ideals and visions of glory, only to find yourself undone by all the undoing, and asking moot questions such as, "Why did I ever start?"

Transitional stages of life are rarely smooth and always stressful. Even when the change is desired and welcomed, the unforeseen complications can deplete and defeat us.

For example, I realized the move would bring quite an adjustment for my son. Since I could foresee that potential problem area, I managed to head it off at the pass. I must say my strategies worked like a charm. I was downright proud of myself.

But then, there were the things I could not foresee that I had budgeted no energy for. I couldn't foresee that the seller from whom I had been buying my house on land contract would attempt to repossess my home on a technicality. I couldn't foresee that my husband's ex-wife would add new dimensions of meaning to the term *uncooperative*. I couldn't foresee a bout with mysterious dizzy spells. And I couldn't foresee that my pets would be traumatized by the change in their territory, adding new, creative hassles to my daily agenda.

Transitional times usually leave things in a bit of a mess.

I know a young woman who was raised in a home which had very strict, rigid requirements on the details of how

Christians should practice the directive to "be not of the world." Through much agonizing soul-searching and much, much prayer she reached a decision to change—not her values or convictions, but her dress, some of her activities, and her church membership. Two years ago she was suicidally depressed. Today she is vibrant, growing, and glowing. Her relationship with God is stronger, her relationship with her husband is closer, her relationships with friends are healthier, and her witness for Christ is much richer and far more effective.

Her relationship with her mother, however, is a mess. That doesn't mean she made wrong choices. It's just that in the transition she's done a lot of undoing and it will take time to put things back together.

Sometimes as individuals make inroads into lifestyle changes and self-improvement plans, they begin to feel that they are getting worse, not better. Times of transition look that way. Think about the last time you tackled that closet in your house (you know, the one where everything gets stashed). With the closet door closed, the room may be neat as a pin. But as you begin the cleaning, sorting, and reorganizing you wind up with...stuff everywhere. No longer neat, the room is now a mess.

If you are in a time of transition, don't be fooled or intimidated by the mess. It is normal. No one can pull off a major life change mess-free.

Remember to allow yourself to accept help. In my transition from one home to another, we have had highlighted for us that some tasks simply cannot be accomplished alone.

Whatever you do, don't abandon the process, but budget some breaks into it. God really knew what he was doing by building a day of rest into our week. Don't let seven days pass without some sort of sabbathing, and be sure to use that sabbath space to replenish, rather than deplete, your energy supply.

I had a seminary professor whose favorite cliché was: "In the Bible it says, 'And it came to pass....' Thank God it didn't come to stay!"

Take heart. In times of transition, things usually look worse before they get better.

Good Intentions and the Path to Hell

"The pathway to hell is paved with good intentions!" I can hear my mother's words echo in my ears as I rummage through the rubble of last year's New Year's resolutions...

First there were the birthday cards. It was a great idea. I *intended* to send them out to everyone on my congregation. My strategy, however, broke down by August.

Then of course there's the ten pounds I *intended* to lose. I make the same resolution every year. And every year it unravels somewhere between Valentine's Day and Easter.

Next on the list are the books I *intended* to read. It's really an impressive line-up of titles. It boggles my mind to consider how smart I'd be if I actually read them!

Finally I consider the projects I *intended* to start: the upholstery that needs cleaning, the pants that need hemming, and the shelves that need stripping.

Why, oh, why is it that "the best laid schemes of mice and men gang aft a-gley; an' lea'e us naught but grief and pain?" I know the answer to that question. And (with all due respect to mom) it's got nothing to do with hell.

It's got to do, first of all with the fact that all too often we make such resolutions based, not upon what we really want to do, but upon what we think we ought to want to do. Take my projects, for instance. (Please! Take them!)

I should know better than to make resolutions that require advanced sewing, cleaning, elbow grease, or artistic talent. I'm totally intimidated by that stuff! What's more, there are people who enjoy such things and who actually earn their living doing them. So for next year, I've resolved that I will improve the economy by providing work for them.

As for the list of theological and clinical journals? If I ever decide to pursue a doctoral degree, I'm sure someone will see to it that my mind gets improved by such reading. But for the time being, I'm a pastor, not a professor. And while I may have forfeited academic challenges this past year, I did manage to read through the *Chronicles of Narnia* with my son. So this year's reading resolutions gets adjusted to more pleasure and joint reading.

The second reason we flounder at our resolutions is a matter of perspective...a variation of the old adage as to whether the glass is half-full or half-empty.

For example, the birthday cards. True, I didn't make it through the whole year. But I did make it through more than half the year. And it's still a great idea. That one stays for next year.

As you review your own list of New Year's resolutions, my guess is that for the things you didn't do, you'll find that one or both of the reasons mentioned above is why.

If you realize you made a resolution according to someone else's agenda, then it's time to define your own desires and adjust your aspirations accordingly.

If you started out strong and finished weak, then your solution lies in "...try, try again." Chances are, you did make progress and just need to remember Galatians 6:9: "Let us not grow weary in doing what is right, for we will reap at harvest-time, if we do not give up."

So if you look behind you and see a trail of discarded resolutions, it's time to reexamine your motives and refocus your goals. That way you can turn the good intentions on the path at your feet into stepping stones for growth.

THE LOCKED DOOR

I spotted it as I was rushing through the parking lot on a gray November day: a dark blue sedan nestled between two pickup trucks, empty of occupants, with its lights on.

"What would Jesus do?" I asked myself—a question that didn't take long to answer. I shifted toward the car with intervention on my mind.

It wasn't an old car. It wasn't a new car. It wasn't a luxury car. It wasn't a klunker. It was just an average, ordinary, made-in-America car with slightly worn vinyl, a few rust spots, tires that had seen many miles...and locked doors.

I briefly considered the possibility that it belonged to some eccentric millionaire who had equipped it with one of those loud, embarrassing alarms. Then I tried all the doors just to make sure. Nothing happened. No alarm sounded, no owner appeared, no doors opened, and no lights got turned off.

As I walked away—a good Samaritan wannabe—I couldn't help but compare my thwarted attempt at intervention with the car to people situations...

I remember as a probation officer sitting across from many a hostile teenager who desperately needed what I had to offer, but the doors were locked.

In marriage counseling, I've had more than a few spouses glare at me across a sea of suspicion. I deeply cared about the fate of their marriage. I knew what needed to be done...and I knew how to do it. But the doors were locked.

Countless times I've listened to myself explain the dynamics of addiction to one entangled in its web. I identified the symptoms. I confronted the behavior. I recommended treatment. But the doors were locked.

I've watched helplessly as people I love careen down a course of self-destruction. I could see the damaging choices.

I could foresee the inevitable consequences. I desperately wanted to help. Bu the doors were locked.

No doubt the owner of the car came back to a dead battery. And the time and effort required to fix that problem was far more costly than the time and effort it would've taken to turn off the lights had the doors not been locked.

"But," you say, "the doors needed to be locked for protection."

Maybe so with the car. But more often than not, with people, locked doors have more to do with a *perceived* need for protection than an *actual* need for protection. That's how we arrive at the term *defensive* when people bristle at the slightest comment, i.e., they *feel* an attack where none is intended.

And, very much like the car, locked doors preventing intervention will lead to dead batteries that require more taxing work later.

There was a time I might've worked harder to find the owner of the car. But you know, even the good Samaritan knew his limits (see Luke 10). He did what he could do to help, then moved on.

When we do not have the key to our possession, we have to accept our own powerlessness where locked doors are concerned. We can try. We can watch. We can pray. We can wait. But in order to intervene, the door has to be unlocked from the inside.

Shifting Gears

My husband is employed by Daimler-Chrysler, whose Kokomo divisions produce virtually all the transmissions for the Chrysler vehicles made in the United States. That's a lot of transmissions. Consequently, Chrysler never closes. The plants in Kokomo operate 24/7, 365 days a year.

New hires are nearly always assigned to the second shift, appropriately nicknamed "the no-life shift." So when Horst first started we were resigned to him working 3:00 p.m. to 11:00 p.m. until he gained enough seniority to "hold" first…a process that can take many months, if not years.

However, to our very pleasant surprise, after just four months he was transferred from his second shift job to a first shift position. The not-so-pleasant part of the surprise was realizing the degree to which the boys and I had adapted to afternoons and evenings without him. Suddenly he's back— disrupting our routine and bringing with him some ridiculous expectations about certain things.

Like dinner, for instance. It had become a rather fluid concept for the three of us. (Why on earth would I cook for two teenage boys, one who always wants to have pizza and the other who always wants to be gone?) And now Horst comes home and, of all things, expects a meal in the evening!

There's also the breaches of parental protocol. On more than one occasion Horst has told the kids not to do something I'd been allowing in his absence, as well as approving other activities I'd previously vetoed. He has trouble remembering one of the cardinal rules of parental permission-giving, i.e., when a teenager asks to do something always get some basic information before saying yes: "Have you finished your homework? Taken care of your laundry? Done all of your chores? Where are you going and with whom? Does their family have HBO, or any other off-limits channels?

Does this kid have a recent drug screen on file? Have I ever seen his or her picture hanging in the post office?" Kids, of course, possess the strategical genius of Napoleon when it comes to maneuvering around these interparental communication gaps.

And then there's bedtime. Not the kids'—ours. Since Horst hadn't been getting home till after midnight, I'd been staying up later myself, reading. Now just because his alarm goes off at 4:45 a.m., he's in bed by 10 p.m., wanting *me* to turn off the light!

According to the dictionary, the transmission consists of "the gears by which power is transmitted from the engine of an automobile to the axle that propels the vehicle." It's a converter, a connector. It makes different parts work together. Too bad there's not a transmission to help different parts of a household work together.

Keep in mind, my husband's move from second shift to first was a much-desired change. We *wanted* our life together back. We *rejoice* in a more normal schedule and consider it a blessing to be able to function again as a family. But change—even when it's positive, even when it's desirable— requires adjustments. It takes some gear shifting in order for things to run smoothly.

If you are growing as a person, if you are growing as a church, then change is your constant companion. And we have to remember that even the good and necessary changes will at first feel uncomfortable. Because of that, we can't allow our comfort level to be the gauge as to whether or not the change is *right*. Our gauge is not how something *feels* to us. On a personal level, our gauge is whether or not a particular change is in our best interests. On a corporate level, our gauge is whether or not a particular change is in keeping with our church's overall mission.

There's no doubt in my mind that my husband working first shift instead of second is better for our family. But that doesn't mean the change was easy. We had to shift gears to make it work.

COOKIES ON THE CUTTING EDGE

My son Jameson loves cut-out Christmas cookies. I love them too—when somebody else makes them!

Don't get me wrong—I enjoy baking. And I'm all for holiday traditions. It's just that the task of making cut-out cookies carries a large fuss factor and I don't have the patience and finesse to do the job right. However, I also don't possess the emotional fortitude to resist his hopeful "Please, Mom!" So for most of his sixteen Christmases we've tackled the task of cut-out Christmas cookies.

What makes the whole project even more frustrating for me is that—assuming they're all evenly rolled, transferred to the cookie sheet in one piece, and not burnt around the edges during baking—by the time the frosting is on them, they're virtually unrecognizable! Which leaves me feeling that all that extra effort was wasted.

While wrestling with this baker's "catch 22" several years ago, I had a flash of inspiration and exclaimed, "Hey, Jameson, let's frost some of them on the back this time. That way we can still tell what they're supposed to be."

My son's face looked about as enthusiastic as the fatted calf's must've been upon the prodigal's return. All he said was, "Not!"

You see, we'd never done it that way before.

However, since I am still the mom, I pulled rank and we did it my way. And you know what? They turned out okay. They weren't the works of art you'd find in a bakery. And they weren't as sharply defined as E.L. Fudge cookies (I suspect the Keebler elves have better equipment). And they probably wouldn't have brought top dollar at the church bake sale.

But they were recognizable. The angels looked like heavenly host instead of heavenly ghosts. The familiar etchings on Santa's face remained visible so he didn't look like a warped daisy. It was easy to tell the lions from the lambs.

The shepherds, wisemen, and snowmen maintained their separate identities. And I was especially pleased that the baby in the manger looked much more like a baby than a confectioner's rendition of E.T.

We altered a tradition. Maybe we even improved upon it. The earth didn't move. The sky didn't fall. The communists didn't get us. And I don't think we gave the devil a foothold. We simply experimented with a different way to accomplish our mutual objectives. Maybe we'll do it again next year. Maybe we won't.

We recently crossed the threshold into the twenty-first century. So considering that we're at the very brink of the new millennium, I'd like to make a suggestion: Experiment with new ways of thinking:

Consider, if only for the sake of argument, that the opposition to your pet issue has some valid points.

Consider that maybe, just *maybe*, your understanding of that particular passage of Scripture is not the only way to look at it.

Consider the possibility that your theology is a reflection of your biases, and not vice versa.

Consider that perhaps long-held beliefs and attitudes are more a product of tradition than convention.

Maybe your diet will flounder by Valentine's Day. Maybe this won't be the year you kick smoking. Maybe after a week of headaches you'll reach for a cup of coffee. Maybe your new exercise regime won't survive January's sub-zero temperatures.

But even if all the rest of your good intentions and resolutions fall by the wayside, clear the cobwebs out of your attitudes. Try icing some cut-out cookies on the back instead of the front. It's just a teensy, weensy risk. If you do nothing else this century, try something you've never tried before, and allow yourself to be transformed by the renewing of your mind (Rom. 12:2).

Raking Uphill

I was out raking leaves a couple of weeks ago.

Time out. Perhaps I'd better explain. Some people don't *do* windows. Some don't *do* sushi. I don't *do* yard work. It's not that I'm too proud or prissy or anything like that. Frankly, it intimidates me. I suppose it comes from growing up in a family where sex-role stereotyping was the determining factor for chore assignments. None of my four brothers were ever made to *do* dishes or laundry and I was never made to *do* garbage or yard work. It's really left us all quite handicapped.

And fortunately for me (though unfortunately for my neighbors) I have a very high tolerance for weeds, crab grass, and dead leaves. As you can imagine, raking has simply not been a regular part of my fall routine.

However, several days ago I realized that the leaves in my yard were blowing over onto the carpet-like grass next door. So I decided that perhaps one of the specific ways I could go about loving my neighbor as myself might be to rake and bag my leaves. Hence my initiation into yard work.

It wasn't bad at all. Once I got the hang of it I actually enjoyed it. But while I was laboriously and methodically hacking away at those brown, brittle, little leaves, I realized I was doing something incredibly counterproductive. I was raking uphill.

The physical sciences are far and away not my area of expertise. But I do remember something about gravity. So it didn't take much to figure out I was making my job a lot harder than it had to be.

I think Christians are notorious for raking uphill in the lawn of life. How many times do you make things harder than they have to be?

Many, many women, when invited somewhere for a meal, simply cannot allow themselves to show up empty-handed no matter how emphatically they are told they need not bring anything. They insist upon just "throwing a little something together." If you ask me, that's raking uphill.

Having functioned all my adult life in one or another branch of the helping professions, I've seen firsthand a lot of uphill raking in the workplace. For instance, I've known countless, conscientious workers who refused to turn in expenses incurred in job-related activities or overtime spent in a crisis situation. They insisted upon raking uphill.

I know a very dear, delightful woman who, when there is a lull in business at her place of employment, feels obligated to detract those minutes from her timecard. She's raking uphill.

One person shared with me how she'd been wanting to get started in a 12-Step group but was intimidated by the thought of going to the meeting alone the first time. "Couldn't you go with the friend who told you about it?" I asked. "Yes, but I feel it's a cop-out to call her. I should be able to do it alone." To which I replied, "I don't know if you should or shouldn't, but if you feel the need for support and it's available, accept it." Why rake uphill?

Theologically, too many who are poor in spirit are bound to rake uphill. One young client told me, between sobs, that she wanted to get right with God because she was so afraid of going to hell: "But I feel that's not a good enough reason. It's like using God." After swallowing the lump in my throat I said to her, "I don't think God minds being used in that way. He accepts you right where you are, regardless of your motive." For heaven's sake, don't rake uphill.

I don't know where Christians ever got the idea that *harder* and *better* are synonymous. True enough, sometimes the hard way is the best way. But too many other times uphill raking doesn't get a job done better. It doesn't make something more righteous or noble. It doesn't gain appreciation or gratitude. It just plain makes things harder.

There are plenty of situations in life when we aren't given easy choices. So then it makes sense to remember that when we are given the option of a legitimate course of action that is smoother and less complicated, taking the easy way is probably the better way.

Since I don't have an ascetic bone in my body, when I realized I was making my task more difficult by raking uphill, I switched directions. Maybe you should too.

STREP AND STEWARDSHIP

It started on Saturday night—the tightness in my throat and the congestion in my head. By Sunday morning it was agony to swallow. The chilling in my bones and the throbbing behind my eyes told me I had a fever before the thermometer did.

I wanted to crawl back in bed. *Ordinary people*, I told myself, *could crawl back into bed on Sunday morning. But not pastors. I mean, how can church happen without the preacher? The show must go on, right?*

So I took some aspirin, stuffed my purse with throat lozenges and tissues, picked up my cross, and resolutely set my face towards the east.

I got through it, of course. Perhaps with less energy than usual, but passable. Few even suspected.

The fever climbed all afternoon. By evening it was 102 and there were suspicious-looking white spots on my throat. But since pastors sometimes operate under the delusion that we are indispensable, I rallied with a nap and more aspirin to lead Bible study that night.

Now, I knew it was strep before the throat culture confirmed it the next day. "By the way," my doctor said as I left his office, "strep is highly contagious. Stay away from people until you've been on the medication for twenty-four hours."

"Highly contagious.... Stay away from people..." The words rang in my ears like an indictment as my mind flooded with images of all the hands I had shaken following worship after coughing into my own.

I went home and looked up "strep infection." There, down at the bottom of the page, were the words, "possible complications: rheumatic fever...serious effects if left untreated...permanent heart damage...susceptible, children and elderly."

I thought of Alice—frail, struggling, ninety-year-old Alice who is so faithful in church despite failing health—whose cheek I had kissed Sunday morning. I thought of Vera—Vera with the heart transplant—for whom any infection carries scary complications. I thought of the children whose faces I had leaned right down into. I thought of the dozens of people I had put at risk because of my determination to minister.

The point here is not a refresher course on strep infection. The point is a principle that I have taught to hundreds of others, but have never had hit me so squarely in my pride: If I do not take care of myself, I risk hurting others.

It's true. Run the whole gamut of behavior choices and you won't find an exception.

Take the mother who deprives herself of sleep, baking elaborately decorated cookies in order to impress her son's fellow preschoolers (who would be just as happy with vanilla wafers). The next day, she's inefficient at work, insensitive to her kids, and irritable with her husband. By not taking care of herself, she winds up hurting others.

Consider the man who notices blood in his stool but fails to get to the doctor to have it checked out. "I can't afford to lose the time at work; the doctor makes you wait for hours. And besides, I don't get sick leave, and my family can't get by without my paycheck." So by the time the colon cancer is diagnosed, it's spread too far to fight. Looks like his wife and kids will have to learn to get by without his paycheck after all. He didn't take care of himself and others got hurt.

And what about the untold numbers who ignore emotional and relational needs? "Counseling is expensive," they stubbornly rationalize.

"So are caskets," says my dear friend who lost her sister to suicide.

"Not as expensive as divorces," say the multitudes who learned the hard way.

No matter how strong the commitment, no matter how pure the motives, no matter how noble the call, for Christians the bottom line is that our bodies, our selves, are not our own. We have been bought with a price. We honor God when we take care of ourselves (1 Cor. 7:20, paraphrased). That's not selfishness, friends, that's stewardship. If we do not take care of ourselves, somebody else is going to get hurt.

BUYING TIME

There it was again: chirping—desperate, panic-stricken chirping. I stopped jogging and looked across the road in time to see a cat darting behind some shrubs, while up above—flying low—was what appeared to be a family of anxious robins.

A sick feeling came over me as I realized the cat had a bird in its clutches. I froze with indecision, listening to the periodic distress signal of the captured fledgling and watching the helpless flurry of its parents and siblings each time it cried.

"Save the baby!" screamed my maternal instinct.

"Only the strong survive," whispered an echo of Darwin.

"But that cat is somebody's well-fed pet!" argued my ethics.

"It's probably too late anyway," the pessimist in me replied.

I turned to move on when the bird cried again, and something inside of me snapped: *The strong should help the weak—not eat them.* So I moved toward the bushes.

This was not easy for me. The sight of blood makes me faint. So as I drew closer to the sounds I felt my stomach heave. I saw the cat first—a gray tabby. She was crouched about eighteen inches from the bird, who appeared to be totally unharmed. Keeping the cat at bay I scooped up the baby robin, carried it a stone's throw away and let it flutter off. Then I bodily transported the cat to her owner several houses down the block. With my mission accomplished I jogged off into the sunset humming the theme to *Rocky*.

That is not, however, the end of the story. The fact of the matter is, I don't know the end of the story. The poor little bird may yet have died of shock. Another predator may have caught it before it recovered enough to get off the ground. And though I sternly instructed the cat to stay home, I've no doubt she slunk back at the first opportunity.

The world was still full of dangers for one little robin who had just left the nest. I didn't save the bird at all. All I did was buy it some time.

Remembering that bird keeps me humble. Because as a pastor, sometimes I want to be a savior...as a counselor, sometimes I want to be a savior...as a parent, sometimes I want to be a savior.

Many, many roles in life can seduce us into believing we are saviors. And, at least for me, it is stabilizing to remember that no matter how skilled, determined, insightful, inspired, or prophetic I may be when I intervene in the lives of others, more often than not my contribution boils down to creating a temporary pocket of safety that buys them some time...time to recover and get strong enough to fly on their own.

And that is honorable work, friends. In an age when being Enabler and Rescuer top the list of relational sins, we can be intimidated into a posture of paralysis where others are concerned. Codependency notwithstanding—there are situations where buying time for another means the difference between victory or defeat...life or death...heaven or hell. Take my little feathered friend, for instance. He would have undoubtedly been...well...dead meat, had I not responded to his SOS.

It's a limited role, but a valuable one. We're not saviors. But buying time, i.e., creating temporary pockets of safety for those in crisis, can make a world's worth of difference in a life...and a life's worth of difference in the world.

PENNY-WISE, BLESSING POOR

I'm a penny pincher.

When my car needs gas, I pull in to the station that has the lower price. It doesn't matter which side of the street; it doesn't matter who has the cleaner restrooms. I go for the pennies saved.

When I compare canned goods at the grocery, I make my decision based upon which costs a cent or two less.

When I see a penny on the street, I pick it up. Never mind about good luck, I simply deposit it in my penny jar and let them add up.

And when I stop at my local convenience store and hand the cashier a dollar bill and a nickel for the ninety-nine cent soda, I never relinquish my penny change to the little penny pool on the counter that says, "Need a penny? Take one. Have a penny? Leave one." A penny saved is a penny earned, I've always figured.

Until recently.

I was one of those hot, sticky Indiana summer days. I made a routine pit stop and filled my thirty-two-ounce cup with diet pop. But as I stepped into line at the check-out, I was dismayed to find in my wallet only four quarters, three pennies, and a twenty-dollar bill. My eyes landed on the little container of copper by the cash register.

What a dilemma! I hated to break a twenty for lack of a penny. Yet, since it had not been my habit to contribute to the penny pot, the thought of accepting a penny tortured my pride and triggered my guilt.

As the line got shorter my moment of reckoning got closer.

"That'll be a dollar four, puh-leeze."

No one watching knew that a mountain had just been scaled...a chasm had been crossed...a dragon had been slain. Without flinching I slipped my finger into the tray and accepted the unearned, unmerited gift.

Remember "the words of the Lord Jesus...'It is more blessed to give than to receive'" (Acts 20:35b). How many times have we heard it? But let's also remember some other words of the Lord Jesus: "Freely you have received, freely give" (Matt.10:8b, NIV). Notice the progression there—the ability to give freely is directly connected to having received freely.

I suspect my crossroad at the convenience store is very much like the crossroads many face day in and day out. Those who have not received will have difficulty giving.

The one who's never received affirmation seldom gives affirmation.

The one who's never received forgiveness seldom gives forgiveness.

The one who's never received love is incapable of giving love.

Our culture presents us with many occasions for gift giving. There are the long-established ones—Christmas, Valentine's Day, Mother's and Father's Days, birthdays, and anniversaries. Then there are a number of not-so-well-known special days which retailers tell us require gift giving—Sweetest Day, Grandparents' Day, Secretaries Day, Boss Day (my brother Mark refers to these as "The Hallmark Conspiracy").

By the time you add weddings, graduations, promotions, and retirements to the list, barely a week goes by without us having to make a decision about whether or not to give a gift to someone. Some give lavishly on every occasion. Some give sparingly on selected occasions. And if you fit into the latter category, perhaps it's time to evaluate your RQ (Receiving Quotient).

When was the last time you let another treat you to lunch?

Have you allowed someone to return a favor lately?

Are you sure you spent that last gift certificate from your in-laws on yourself?

Have you accepted a compliment without trying to argue the giver out of it?

If you haven't received freely, you'll be impaired in your ability to give freely.

I still buy cheap gas. I still have a jar for collecting loose change. But now I leave pennies in the little containers beside cash registers. It'll never heal the sick, feed the hungry, or save the lost, but in some small way it has set this captive free. My crossroad at the convenience store stands as my personal pilgrimage, teaching me that once I allow myself to receive, I am free to give.

VI TOWARD HIGHER GROUND

Setting your mind on things above

FLOODS AND FAITH

I live in an area that knows seasonal flooding. Every spring the local waterways overflow, creating detours, invading basements, and generally wreaking havoc. Along with the sump pumps and sandbags that appear, it seems like every news reporter and broadcaster suddenly becomes a crisis counselor wannabe: "Keep an emergency kit handy...turn off electrical appliances...switch to battery operated...carry a flashlight.... store bottled water...discard canned food that has been damaged...abandon stalled cars immediately...if you're driving and you come to a flooded area, turn around and go another way" (duh!).

The significant thing I notice, though, is that one piece of advice consistently offered by everyone is: "Move to higher ground."

What makes sense in the physical world works spiritually as well. Throughout our lives we have countless junctures when our path is flooded with trials and tribulations. We are engulfed with stress, tempted by sin, discouraged by disappointments, frustrated with results, and blocked by failure. Often we can find a way to cope...discover a detour...learn to wade through.

But sometimes no amount of analyzing, processing, reframing, or discussing seems to help. That's when we move to higher ground spiritually; we set our sights on things above and remember that this world is not our eternal home and life's afflictions will not last forever.

"When you pass through the waters, I will be with you" (Isa. 43:2*a*).

God doesn't promise that we'll avoid the waters, only that he'll be with us. The higher ground of the Christian call helps us to transcend present circumstances and live above life's disappointments.

> *Lord lift me up and let me stand*
> *By faith on heaven's tableland;*
> *a higher plane than I have found*
> *Lord, plant my feet on higher ground.*
> —Johnson Oatman, Jr.

The Gospel According to Seashells

Although it was Horst's first trip to Florida, it wasn't mine. I have a number of beaches in my past: Clearwater with my parents and brothers...Daytona just out of high school...Cocoa Beach during college spring breaks...Smyrna Beach as a youth group sponsor...visits to friends in West Palm. But in none of those previous trips to beaches did I ever bother to gather seashells.

Hence, I did not realize that the vast majority of shells washed up on the beach are already broken. And since we were looking for the big, clean, beautiful shells they sell in souvenir shops, the pastime that began as "Let's take some-thing home to the kids" gradually evolved into a quest for perfection. As a result we found ourselves bending, crawling, digging, and diving—anything to find the perfect shell, the Holy Grail, the pearl of great price.

And you know what we got out of it? Aching backs, bro-ken nails, skinned knees, and sunburned shoulders. Not even one unbroken shell of any size.

Something more important happened during the process, though. Sifting through the sand forced me to notice the less-than-perfect shells. The longer I looked, the less imperfection became a point for disqualification. I felt myself increasingly drawn toward the broken shells that were colorful, unique, and interesting.

Which are the very same qualities that attract me to people.

Shells are not geological accidents, but rather the remains of what once was a living being. Consequently, their very brokenness stands as a tangible testimony giving clues to their history.

Like people.

The rich, true colors spoke to me of life more abundant (see John 10:10). The irresistible iridescence reminded me of the light of the knowledge of God in the face of Christ (2 Cor. 4:6). And the contrast between the outer mud-colored roughness and the inner mother-of-pearl smoothness underscored the eternal tragedy of judging another by outward appearance, for the Lord looks at the heart (1 Sam. 16:7).

You see, once I discarded perfection as a criterion for acceptance I began to see all kinds of beauty in broken shells. So with even greater ambition than I scrounged for perfect shells, I began adopting broken shells…big broken shells, little broken shells, many broken shells. In my transition of perception, the brokenness came to add to, rather than detract from, their value.

Like people.

The dilemma we faced upon returning from our honeymoon with bags full of memories was figuring out what to do with them. So like good little tourists we bought one of those "designer" lamp kits with a clear glass base—you know, like you find in Wal-Mart. The white sands of St. Andrews State Park cushion the bottom, and the rest is filled with the broken shells from the beaches of Panama City. I doubt that you'll ever see one featured in Martha Stewart's_magazine, but we like it.

Then, as we filled up the base with our shells, the real miracle happened: In a group, you can no longer tell they're broken. Nestled against each other like the interlocking pieces of a jigsaw puzzle, this one's jagged edge is covered by that one's scalloped edge. The hole in one is filled by a glint of color from the one behind it. Two missing pieces side by side blend together creating the image of wholeness.

So when we look at our lamp, instead of seeing a jar full of broken shells, we see a colorful, cooperating collage of a complete community.

Like people.

Had I insisted upon perfection, I'd have come away disappointed and frustrated. Instead, my broken shells provide a visible symbol of an invisible grace...an enduring metaphor of how broken people come together, enhancing each others' strengths and compensating for each others' weaknesses to provide Light to a hurting world.

My Husband, the Junkie

It was 5:30 a.m. and the clock radio had just switched on. My husband was crawling back into bed after taking our fourteen-year-old to an early morning commitment.

"Guess what?" he said.

The excitement in his voice was cause for immediate concern.

"What?" I said cautiously.

"You know that little back street we cut through on to get to the church? Well, one of the houses had some stuff sitting out for the trash. I stopped and looked and there was a Eureka vacuum cleaner, so I brought it home. The fan belt had broken and gotten sucked up and jammed into the impeller. I pulled it out and cleaned the motor. It works fine. And there was a water softener that just needs a timer and cam assembly. They also had three chairs with oak sides sitting out. The upholstery's dirty, but I can clean that. There was a cute little metal chair missing a seat so I picked it up and brought it home too. And there was a bicycle with a wrecked frame and bent tires, but the gear shifters and cables are still good."

All of this before 5:30 a.m.?! I started laughing and said, "You need help!"

Even though the boys and I tease him mercilessly about his junk-aholism, to be honest, I respect it. In a world of disposable towels, disposable dinnerware, disposable jobs, disposable relationships, and disposable values there is something both endearing and redemptive about someone who loves to rescue, repair, and use broken things.

I recall seeing during my freshman year of college a low-budget animated film that was produced to encourage conservation and recycling. It showed people all over the world throwing things away until little by little everyone was practically drowning in trash. In the final frame of the film we saw the Earth hanging in space and overflowing with trash. As more and more trash spilled into the universe, a huge hand from heaven entered the picture, grabbed the Earth, wadded it up, and threw it away.

Do you suppose that's what the old spiritual means by its hook line: "He's got the whole world in his hands"?

In one way or another we're all broken: We're angry, we're uptight, we're cynical, we're insecure, we're selfish, we're jealous...the list is endless. And no matter the specifics of how you continue that list, the irrefutable truth is that something in us doesn't work right: our upholstery's dirty, our motor is jammed, our frame is bent.

While the film from my college days undoubtedly made its environmental point, the good news of gospel is that God doesn't trash us. Instead of just wadding us up with his heavenly hand and dumping us into some cosmic landfill, God sent his son to save us.

My husband's rescue operation has had substantial dividends. The little metal ice cream parlor chair has a fresh coat of white paint, a new mauve seat, and looks adorable in the corner of our bedroom. The three oak chairs are now serving a Baptist Sunday school class across town. The salvaged bicycle shifters and cables are an improvement on my old Schwinn. The restored water softener is fully operational, providing both soft water and an increase in our property value. The repaired vacuum cleaner has been adopted by a family who really needed it.

For many of us, Christianity is about newness—new covenant, new life, new birth. But it occurs to me that Christianity is also about old things, people with broken hearts, wounded spirits, and tainted lives being rescued, repaired, and put to good use by the One who indeed has the whole world in his hands.

WAR IS A GOOD IDEA

War is such a good idea.

Think about it: The quest to protect the innocent, punish the wicked, and defeat evil is so terribly noble and righteous.

War is a good idea.

Not long ago I watched the action film *True Lies* (living with all males, I usually get outvoted on which videos to rent). But in this film, a woman discovers that her mild-mannered husband is secretly a special agent in government affairs. During a moment of horrifying revelation, she asks her husband, "Do you mean you've actually *killed* people?"

"Well, yes," he says meekly, then hurries to add this disclaimer, "but they were all bad guys!"

You've got to admit, bad guys getting their just deserts is a *good* idea. Now all that's left for us to do is figure out who the bad guys are.

Let's see…

The conservatives think the liberals are the bad guys. Pro-life activists consider pro-abortionists bad guys. The Ku Klux Klan thinks all nonwhite, non-Protestants are the bad guys. Some heterosexual people refer to homosexual people as the bad guys.

The Palestinians think the Israelis are the bad guys. The Serbs believe the Armenians are the bad guys. Capitalists would say communists are the bad guys.

Wait a minute—that's all true in reverse as well.

The Jews in the first century believed the Christians were the bad guys. The Catholics considered the Reformers to be the bad guys. The Reformers, in turn, defined the Anabaptists as the bad guys. The Nazis named the Jews as the bad guys.

This is ridiculous! How are we supposed to have a war when we can't figure out who the bad guys are?

I watched a *Star Trek, Next Generation* rerun not long ago that delivered a powerful message. Captain Jean Luc Piccard was held prisoner by a Cardacien who was torturing him just for the perverted pleasure and sense of superiority it gave him. During one interlude, the Cardacien's little daughter came in and asked her father, "Daddy, do humans have families like us?"

He said to her, "Well, sweetheart, they do. But humans don't love their children nearly as much as we do."

It looks like all it takes to be a bad guy is for someone else to decide you are.

Maybe war *isn't* such a good idea.

In answer to a question, Albert Einstein replied: "I do not know how World War III will be fought. But I *do* know how World War IV will be fought—with sticks and stones." And Martin Luther King, Jr. said, "We must all learn to live together as brothers [and sisters] or perish together as fools."

So if war can't get rid of the bad guys and give us a solution to evil, what can?

"I bring you the most joyful news ever announced, and it is for everyone! The Savior—yes the Messiah, the Lord—has been born tonight in Bethlehem!... 'Glory to God in the highest heaven...and peace on earth for all those pleasing him'" (Luke 2:10-14, LB).

War sounds like a good idea, until we realize that at some point or another, *everybody* is *somebody's* bad guy. Jesus Christ is the good news for bad guys everywhere: He "gave himself for our sins, that he might deliver us out of this present evil age, according to the will of our God and Father" (Gal.1:4, NASB).

LAWN AND LIFE MAINTENANCE

I helped my husband mow the lawn not too long ago, an event that occurs only slightly more often than the appearance of Halley's Comet. (Like I said, my parents were firm believers in sex-role stereotyping. In my defense let me say that none of my brothers knew how to do laundry when they left home.)

But at first it was kind of fun. That is, until I began surveying my work. We don't have one of those lush, green, *Better-Homes-and-Gardens* lawns. We've got a dirty-colored lawn full of rocks, roots, ridges, and rills.

When I turned to look behind me, I couldn't see where I'd been.

I took off my BluBlocker sunglasses, and I still couldn't see where I'd been.

I got off the tractor and stooped down for a close-up look. And still it was hard to see where I'd been.

I remember that experience often...

I remember it when I hear a mother tell of walking through the house she just cleaned yesterday picking up socks, putting away shoes, and calling for kids who must be wearing blinders and earplugs. She can' t see where she's been.

I remember it as I listen to a divorced father lament the inequities of a legal system whose deeply embedded biases for the custodial parent consistently work against him. After eons of negotiations, miles of red tape, thousands of dollars, and years of trying, he can't see where he's been.

I remember it once again as a disillusioned pastor repeats the old, old story of pouring out his life as a drink offering before a congregation that is long on good intentions and family ties, but short on vision and follow-through. He can't see where he's been.

I remember it every time a kindred spirit tells me of yet another visit to the doctor confirming that the weight, cholesterol, and blood pressure are still high even after weeks of a diet that is low-fat, low-sugar, low-salt, and low-taste. They can't see where they've been.

I am beginning to think that nothing in life carries a higher discouragement risk than the fear that our efforts are in vain.

I find it interesting that tanning salons provide little body decals. Apparently, since so many of the clientele opt to tan—well...all over—the sticker is a way to measure before and after.

Whatever our task—be it serious, silly, routine or ambitious—we need to believe that our work counts for something.

When I mowed the grass, I couldn't tell where I'd been. That is, until my husband pulled me over to view my work from his vantage point. And, low and behold, from a different angle I could indeed see the demarcation between where I had been and where I was going.

That's a valuable lesson. When our energy is low and our frustration is high, it helps to have another perspective. We are usually our own harshest critic. So someone else willing to help us view our work from a different angle can go a long way towards alleviating the suffocating panic that taunts us into believing our efforts are useless.

In the third chapter of 1 Corinthians, the apostle Paul tells us that the Day will bring to the light our work, that it will be shown for what it is, and that fire will test the quality of each one's work. And on the spiritual level, I truly believe that even when we can't see where we've been, God can. And what God sees, counts.

Meanwhile, back on the ranch, I've decided to switch from lawn mowing to tanning!

FAITH AND FANTASY

I'm really not very sophisticated. Or intellectual for that matter. I can wing it when I have to, but for the most part my tastes and outlook on life tend to be quite bourgeois.

I like ketchup with steak and prefer coffee over tea. I can't tolerate seafood unless it's camouflaged by lots of breading. The appeal of Brie cheese is lost on me.

When it comes to movies I never agree with the critics; I like the ones that make me laugh or cry, rather than those that make me *think*. I read *People* magazine on the sly whenever I'm in someone else's waiting room. I don't want to read a novel that doesn't have a happy ending. My definition of classical music is anything from the seventies. (That's *1970*s.) I like for poems to rhyme.

I'm intrigued by the mystique of religious artifacts. I'm fascinated by the possibility of extraterrestrials. I'm convinced there are such things as guardian angels. And if I could get away with it, I'd believe in Santa Claus.

During my college years I aligned myself with a group of zealots (they called us Jesus Freaks back then) who insisted that Santa Claus was not merely overemphasized, but was downright blasphemous and in every way anti-Christian. So for a time I was stoutly opposed to participating in any celebration that included white-bearded, fat men in red suits.

Then I started thinking for myself.

And I realized I bore no animosity whatsoever towards my own parents for lying to me about Jolly Old St. Nick. On the contrary, those years constituted some of my warmest memories.

As I entered graduate school, my classes on early childhood development augmented my instinctive inclinations. I learned that children go through stages of growth in their thinking processes.

More specifically, between the ages of two and seven, when they are not yet capable of understanding the principles underlying various mental operations, children engage in intuitive, or magical thinking. Fantasy and make-believe are an integral part of this stage, which is why cartoons, tooth fairies, leprechauns, and Santa Claus seem *real* to young children. Attempting to skip over this stage by insisting that children forfeit magical thinking and by-pass fantasy would be like expecting a child to read before learning the alphabet. It's about as natural, and possible, as skipping diapers or baby teeth.

More recently I've considered how anything which teaches children that you don't have to see something to believe in it just can't be all bad. We live in a materialistic, rationalistic, reductionistic, scientific culture that has created a myth more deceitful and potentially damaging than Santa Claus, i.e., the myth that if we can't see it, taste it, touch it, measure it, dissect it, isolate it, capture it, or put it on a computer it cannot be real.

Which, when you think about it, is totally irrational, for the very survival of civilization daily pivots upon the indisputable reality of things we can't see...things like love, courage, commitment, honesty, hope, compassion, understanding, and integrity. Somehow I think it helps prepare little minds for such virtues by exercising their ability to believe in things unseen.

As an adult, I believe in a God I have never seen. I accept a Savior whose authenticity cannot be validated by my five senses. I've staked my life on a resurrection that defies all reason and logic. I've anchored my future in a place I have no empirical proof even exists.

I'm not elevating Santa Claus to the level of deity. Neither am I demoting God to the status of fairy tale. However, I am suggesting that in the tapestry of Christmas traditions and priorities perhaps the value of Santa Claus can be understood as laying a foundation which increases the capacity and strengthens the ability to believe in something that cannot be seen. Thus what begins as childhood fantasy becomes a building block—or stepping stone—to faith.

The Psychology of Popsicles

I suppose it's not my responsibility to provide Popsicles for every kid that shows up at my back door. I suppose I could shoo them on home to raid their own refrigerators, manipulate their own parents, and argue with their own siblings about who gets the blue one.

But when the day is hot and the play is hard, passing out Popsicles just seems like the neighborly thing to do. And when I consider that for a little under two dollars I can buy twenty-four rainbow-colored smiles, forty-eight sparkling eyes, and 240 sticky fingers, it seems like a pretty decent return on my investment.

Besides, I want them to *like* me.

Now before you go labeling me "codependent," understand there's a method to my madness.

I believe that one of the best ways for parents to strengthen their kids' resistance to the epidemic social problems of current culture is to allow your home to be the place where the gang hangs out. Give your kids a message loud and clear that their friends, and thus their whole lives, are important to you and supported by you. Let their friends know they are wanted and welcomed. Establishing physical space for them in your home communicates that they also have emotional space in your heart.

That doesn't mean you let them walk all over you. It doesn't mean you become either maid or butler. I, for one, am an equal opportunity mother; I'll give orders to anybody's kid! Yet I find that my son's young friends respond remarkably well to my nonnegotiable guidelines.

For instance, all are expected to deposit Popsicle wrappers and sticks in the trash. I remind them to say please and thank you and I'm sorry just like I do my own. I correct grammar. I do not allow name calling, pretend-smoking, ethnic jokes, or cuss words. As you can see, no discrimination here! Whether they

realize it or not, whether they admit it or not, structure equals
security to kids.

Having kids around is not nearly as intrusive as some parents fear it will be. But it doesn't come without its headaches
either: Accidents sometimes happen...messes usually happen...interruptions inevitably happen...and arguments
always happen. And since patience is not one of my virtues,
it can get on my nerves. Feelings get hurt, knees get scraped,
dogs get loose, toys get broken, projects miss deadlines.

However, while I'll be the first to admit I don't always bat
a thousand, I do attempt to practice what I preach. And at
this stage in the life of my family, that includes creating a climate conducive to congregating for my kid's significant others. I will not always be able to control his choice of friends
over the years, but I can at least connect with them and mon-
itor them.

And I like to think that by passing out Popsicles I'm modeling some worthwhile lessons—like generosity, like "doing unto
others," like sharing out of our abundance, like giving a cup of
cold water in Jesus' name. I'd like to think I'm demonstrating that
adults can be friends and allies, folks who can be depended
upon to meet their needs and trusted to do right by them. I'd like
to think I'm cultivating in them an optimistic outlook that will
predispose their young minds to a hopeful bias, that down the
road no matter how discouraging life becomes they'll believe
that there will be someone they can turn to who cares.

Meanwhile I'm the one responsible for nudging up the
price of Popsicle stock and making the shareholders happy.
And if your kids come home with orange evidence all over
their faces, I'm likely the one responsible for that too.

Happy Hour

We have a wet bar in our house. It must have been something of a fad when the house was built thirty-odd years ago because it's located right next to the kitchen. So even for people whose routine beverage choices would make a wet bar make sense, it's not really necessary. Which means, for us it's *really* unnecessary.

So our wet bar has become a storage bin for dog and cat supplies. Consequently we have rechristened our wet bar "The Pet Bar."

The Pet Bar is concealed behind louvered bi-fold doors. They're in good shape; they don't screech or clatter when they're opened. But they do have a characteristic sliding sound. And it's really interesting to see how the pets at our house react.

Yogi, the twelve-year-old miniature fox terrier, is wise to the ways of the world. He knows what's coming out of The Pet Bar, and he figures since it's not people food there's nothing to get excited about.

Mocha, our five-year-old beautiful-but-stuck-up calico cat, looks upon us humans with such disdain she'd never allow us to see her actually eat something. Heaven forbid we get the idea she needs us or in any way appreciates us.

Then there's the Boys.

The Boys are our nine-month-old kittens. While most animals eat to live, the Boys live to eat. And the instant those doors begin to slide along their tract, two balls of feline fur come streaking into the room. It doesn't matter if they're awakened from their catnap. They don't care if they're interrupted during other important engagements like unrolling the toilet paper or knocking over the wastebasket. They'll even abandon their favorite pastime of tormenting Mocha. When The Pet Bar opens for business, it's happy hour, and they're instantly underfoot, meowing, rubbing, and purring.

These are not pampered pets. They don't get gourmet cuisine in champagne glasses. It's just the same plain, dry, cat food day after day. But, if you could see their ecstasy as the food is being poured into their bowl you'd think I just opened a jar of Russian caviar.

"Jesus said to them, 'My food is to do the will of him who sent me'" (John 4:34). "But solid food is for the mature, for those whose faculties have been trained by practice to distinguish good from evil" (Heb. 5:14).

How do you receive spiritual food? What's your reaction to the weekly sermon, your daily Bible reading, a Sunday school lesson?

Like Yogi? "Been there, done that. If it's nothing fancy don't bother me."

Or do you, like Mocha, consider such fare to apply only to others? Perhaps those of a lesser spiritual stature?

Or have you learned the joy of receiving spiritual food like the Boys? Each time, there's something new, and fresh, and exciting. Even the same lessons over and over bring nourishment and satisfaction.

"Do not work for the food that spoils, but for the food that endures for eternal life, which the Son of Man will give you" (John 6:27*a*).

What Computers Don't Know

"...but you see, ma'am, the computer don't know..."

Usually I let such things slide. Usually I don't consider it my place to correct the grammar of other adults. Usually I just grit my teeth and remind myself that a small error in verb conjugation doesn't destroy the intended meaning of the sentence. Usually.

This time, however, my level of frustration had long since surpassed my threshold of tolerance.

"*Doesn't* know," I interrupted her. "The computer *doesn't* know."

There was just a split second of confused silence, then she went on: "Yes, ma'am, like I said, the computer don' t know that you've been paying more than the scheduled loan amount, and it just went ahead and sent you your coupon book for next year's payments."

Several months previously I had purchased a new television set. Being the conscientious steward that I am I opted to take advantage of the twelve-month interest-free financing. Even though the payments were based upon the assumption of a two-year loan, I had religiously paid enough extra every month to make sure I would have a zero balance at the end of twelve months. The fact that the computer didn't know that was exactly why I was so upset!

I am not antitechnology. While computers intimidate me, I respect them, and I've learned to use and appreciate them. I don't know if I even remember how to write without a word processor! No, I like computers just fine and would hate to have to navigate the complexities of our high-tech world without one.

It's just that, like my experience with the finance company so dramatically illustrates, what computers don't know, *can* hurt me. Computers don't know me and the particular circumstances of my situation. They don't know how to respond to my needs and efforts. Computers don't know how to make exceptions, only how to run programs.

They also don't know the fine tuning of communication. I received a letter recently from an organization wanting to know if we would be having a "church bizarre." While spell check is a grand invention, it is certainly no respecter of homonyms. It will tell us whether or not a word is spelled correctly; it won't tell us whether or not that word makes sense in context.

Computers also don't know about individual identity. Just last week I helped my son type his autobiography. Since he included first, middle, and last names of all five brothers, two parents, and four grandparents, it took a long time to get through the spell check because the computer doesn't know that names are words. That same document contained another error the program couldn't catch: Brandon stated at one point that he loved "fiend trips." While that may well be a correct statement, it was supposed to be "field trips."

And I suppose that's what it all boils down to: When it comes to programming,

computers ruthlessly employ the letter of the law. Which is the same thing we find under the Old Covenant.

The Old Testament law made no provision for unique circumstances, no acknowledgment of individuality, no margin for error. It was, quite literally, set in stone. The New Covenant, however, is not set in stone, but rather signed in blood. While stone is hard, cold, and unyielding, blood is fluid, warm, and alive. Centuries ago the apostle Paul tried to make the Christians at Corinth understand this when he wrote: "...for the letter kills, but the Spirit gives life" (2 Cor. 3:6, NIV).

The system of the law, like computers, can only condemn my faults and ignore my efforts. Grace, on the other hand, can forgive my faults and understand my efforts. Which is exactly why the Word became flesh (John 1:14).

"I realize the computer doesn't know I've been paying ahead" (I said this with a pretty good imitation of patience). "I'm calling because I need to know if there exists a record of my additional payments."

"Oh yes, ma'am! I have it all right here in your file."

I'm glad there was a personal backup for my financial account, and it was not totally at the mercy of a computer system. Likewise, I'm glad there's a personal God behind my spiritual account, and my soul is not at the mercy of a legalistic system.

WHEN THE RAINBOW TOUCHED THE EARTH

I saw something awhile back that I had never seen before and am unlikely to ever see again this side of heaven.

I saw where a rainbow touched the earth.

Springing right out of the horizon and stretching over me like a multicolored McDonald's arch was an entire rainbow with all seven colors clearly visible. For the first time in my life I understood how the legend of the pot of gold at the rainbow's end began. For at the point where this rainbow touched the earth a cylindrical shaft of light encapsulated a young tree so that it glimmered and glowed, and emanated a golden, ethereal light. Every vein on every leaf was discernible, and its silhouette jumped out in sharp contrast to those around it.

I realize that the years and mileage have done their share in blunting my idealism. Things like parades, amusement parks, festivals, and athletic events just don't excite me the way they used to. But the wonders of the sky—snowflakes, lightning, full moons, and shooting stars—still enchant me and draw my eyes heavenward.

This rainbow, this complete rainbow, absolutely mesmerized me.

I stopped jogging and gawked, then looked for someone with whom to share this miracle. There aren't too many people out and about on a gray, misty morning. But I noticed a man, his arms full of Saturday chores, struggling out his back door.

"Didja see the rainbow?" I shouted.

Startled, he glanced up and said "Yeah" in a tone that clearly said "Big deal!" So the spell was broken.

According to Genesis 9, the rainbow made its debut after the flood as a reminder of the everlasting covenant between God and all living creatures. Through the ages, then, the rainbow has become a symbol of promise and hope.

Maybe it's different for you, but in spite of the fact that I believe the promises of God to be true, all too often the manifestation of those promises in my life feels an awful lot like typical Indiana rainbows—faded, partial, elusive.

However, as I stood beneath the glory of that vivid, complete rainbow, and as I witnessed its intersection with the earth and the way it bestowed beauty and wonder upon an insignificant little tree, I reflected upon the New Covenant and its consummation in Jesus Christ.

At Christmastime we are flooded with images both secular and sacred: stars, mangers, angels, mistletoe, reindeer, and snow people. It occurs to me that the rainbow too is an appropriate symbol for the Advent, and I think it's about time Christians reclaimed it from the New Age, the Leprechauns, and the Land of Oz.

Wall Street and Washington can commercialize Christmas to the nth degree. They can spell it with an "X." They can remove nativity scenes from public places. They can elevate pagan rituals over sacred tradition. They can eliminate Bethlehem from the classroom. And they can even refuse to give Jesus air play.

But no matter how diligently they attempt to diffuse the miracle of the season, and no matter how vehemently they attack its message, I am triumphantly aware of the fact that at Christmastime the wonders of the sky draw eyes heavenward and people everywhere are compelled to acknowledge, if not accept, that two thousand years ago at a peculiar, unique, never-to-be-repeated ganglion of history in an obscure little town in the heart of Palestine, eternity intersected time.

And the Rainbow touched the earth.

EPILOGUE

For the twenty years prior to his death in 1990 my father was employed in a white-collar job where he basically pushed a pencil and serviced clients. The main things he liked to do with his hands were shoot baskets and pitch softballs, both of which he did rather well in his younger days.

But even though my dad was not a trained craftsman, he was very much a do-it-yourselfer. My husband is a do-it-yourselfer too, but for different reasons. My husband is a do-it-yourselfer because he doesn't trust anyone else to do a job up to his standards. I suspect my father was a do-it-yourselfer because that pencil-pushing, white-collar job was the sole support of a wife and five kids!

Shortly after my family moved into a new house in 1968, Dad installed stepping stones from our driveway to our front door. It was a nice touch. They looked real quaint, and on Sunday mornings especially helped my mother and Aunt Betty keep from sinking into the ground in their high heels (that was back when they both still wore high heels).

I don't know if my dad read any instructions on installing stepping stones. I don't know if he asked anybody how installing stepping stones was done. I don't know if he'd ever installed stepping stones before that. And I don't know if he used any standards of measurement to decide where to place the stepping stones. But I'm pretty sure the answer to all of those questions is no.

What I do know is that for as long as I can remember those stepping stones have not fit my stride. In order to walk on them I have to adjust my long-legged gait into short, mincing, "girl-steps." Which isn't the end of the world since I'm a girl and it wouldn't kill me to occasionally slow down a bit. My brothers, however, look ridiculous!

But every time I walk on those stepping stones I find myself thinking: *If we ever install stepping stones at our house, I'm going to make sure they fit my stride.*

It's entirely possible that the stepping stones in this book do not fit your stride. Be that the case, I must thank you for your generosity in reading them anyway and wish you Godspeed as you continue your walk of faith.

"Now to him who is able to keep you from falling, and to make you stand without blemish in the presence of his glory with rejoicing, to the only God our Savior, through Jesus Christ our Lord, be glory, majesty, power, and authority, before all time and now and forever. Amen" (Jude 24-25).